A NOTE TO THE TEACHER

This book is one of a series of three coursebooks for years 7, 8 and following features...

- It exactly matches both the content and the spirit of the exemplar scheme of work for Year 7 produced by the Qualifications and Curriculum Authority.
- It consists of 12 units in Year 7, each of which is 7 pages long.
- The first 4 pages consist of content and ensure complete coverage of the revised programme of study. The main keywords are highlighted throughout the text.
- Page 5 consists of a "key word" exercise and a "comprehension" based largely on the nature, history and understanding of scientific ideas.
- Page 6 tests understanding through a literacy exercise and then goes on to develop skills involving the production or interpretation of graphs or data.
- Page 7 is devoted entirely to an investigation related to the particular unit. This can be done instead of actually doing the investigation or may be used alongside it in order to develop the investigative skills appropriate to a Year 7 pupil.
- The work is graded to provide access at level 3 as well as sufficient rigour for level 5 and above. Worksheets at 'Higher' and 'Foundation' level are available for each page of content on our website at www.lonsdalesrg.co.uk to enable further differentiation. In total there are over 300 Key Stage 3 worksheets on this site.
- Wherever possible, due consideration has been given to Language for Learning, Numeracy, ICT, PSHE, Citizenship and Key Skills.
- These course books can stand alone or may be used in conjunction with the QCA Teachers' Guide and exemplar scheme of work.

A NOTE TO THE PUPIL

We're sure that you will enjoy using this course book but to make the most of it....

- Tackle the questions seriously and do them to the best of your ability.
- Try to write your answers in good English using correct punctuation and good sentence construction. Read your answers back to yourself.
- Think carefully about graphical work. Make sure your axes are accurately labelled and your points constructed properly.
- Try to learn (by heart if necessary) what all the key words mean.

Good luck

Katie Whelan

© 2003 LONSDALE. ALL RIGHTS RESERVED. NO PART OF THIS PUBLICATION MAY BE REPRODUCED, STORED IN A RETRIEVAL SYSTEM, OR TRANSMITTED IN ANY FORM OR BY ANY MEANS, ELECTRONIC, MECHANICAL, PHOTOCOPYING, RECORDING, OR OTHERWISE WITHOUT THE PRIOR WRITTEN PERMISSION OF LONSDALE.

CONTENTS

Page No.

CELLS

- 4 The Microscope
- 5 The Structure of Animal and Plant Cells
- 6 Cell Specialisation and the Organisation of Life
- 7 Cell Growth and Reproduction
- 8 Keywords and Comprehension
- 9 Testing Understanding
- 10 Scientific Investigation

REPRODUCTION

- 11 Patterns Of Sexual Reproduction
- 12 The Mechanism Of Human Reproduction
- 13 The Menstrual Cycle And Foetal Reproduction
- 14 Birth Onwards
- 15 Keywords and Comprehension
- 16 Testing Understanding
- 17 Scientific Investigation

ENVIRONMENT AND FEEDING RELATIONSHIPS

- 18 Adaptation to Habitat
- 19 Adaptation to Daily and Seasonal Change
- 20 Feeding Relationships
- 21 Food Webs and Competition between Animals
- 22 Keywords and Comprehension
- 23 Testing Understanding
- 24 Scientific Investigation

VARIATION AND CLASSIFICATION

- 25 Variation in Individuals
- 26 Causes of Variation
- 27 Grouping Animals
- 28 Classification
- 29 Keywords and Comprehension
- 30 Testing Understanding
- 31 Scientific Investigation

ACIDS AND ALKALIS

- 32 Characteristics of Acids and Alkalis
- 33 Hazardous Substances
- 34 Indicators
- 35 Neutralisation and Uses
- 36 Keywords and Comprehension
- 37 Testing Understanding
- 38 Scientific Investigation

SIMPLE CHEMICAL REACTIONS

- 39 Reactions of Acids with Metals
- 40 Reactions of Acids with Carbonates
- 41 Burning
- 42 Fuels
- 43 Keywords and Comprehension
- 44 Testing Understanding
- 45 Scientific Investigation

CONTENTS

PARTICLE MODEL OF SOLIDS, LIQUIDS AND GASES

Page No.

- 46 Solids, Liquids And Gases
- 47 Particle Theory
- 48 Diffusion
- 49 Gas Pressure
- 50 Keywords and Comprehension
- 51 Testing Understanding
- 52 Scientific Investigation

SOLUTIONS

- 53 Mixing Substances
- 54 Distillation
- 55 Chromatography
- 56 Saturated Solutions
- 57 Keywords and Comprehension
- 58 Testing Understanding
- 59 Scientific Investigation

ENERGY RESOURCES

- 60 Burning Fuels
- 61 Fossil Fuels
- 62 Renewable Energy Resources
- 63 Food
- 64 Keywords and Comprehension
- 65 Testing Understanding
- 66 Scientific Investigation

ELECTRICAL CIRCUITS

- 67 Electrical Circuits
- 68 Electric Current
- 69 Parallel Circuits
- 70 Dangers of Electricity
- 71 Keywords and Comprehension
- 72 Testing Understanding
- 73 Scientific Investigation

FORCES AND THEIR EFFECTS

- 74 Force, Mass And Weight
- 75 Upthrust
- 76 Friction
- 77 Stopping Distance Of Vehicles
- 78 Keywords and Comprehension
- 79 Testing Understanding
- 80 Scientific Investigation

THE SOLAR SYSTEM AND BEYOND

- 81 The Earth And The Sun
- 82 The Earth, Sun And Moon
- 83 The Solar System
- 84 Beyond Our Solar System
- 85 Keywords and Comprehension
- 86 Testing Understanding
- 87 Scientific Investigation

Lonsdale Science Revision Guides

THE MICROSCOPE

Cells 1

HISTORICALLY

In 1665 an Englishman called Robert Hooke cut some very thin strips of cork and looked at them using a very primitive microscope. What he saw was lots of little spaces, which he called CELLS because they reminded him of the tiny rooms in which monks live. He was the first person to actually see this, even though he was only looking at where the cells had once been!

The invention of the microscope was a huge technological breakthrough which enabled scientists to develop ideas about the structure of living things.

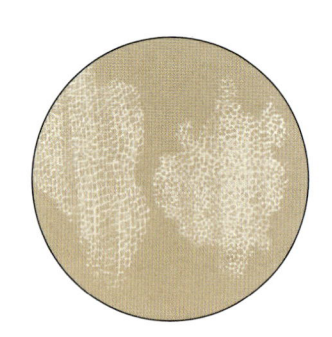

THE MODERN MICROSCOPE

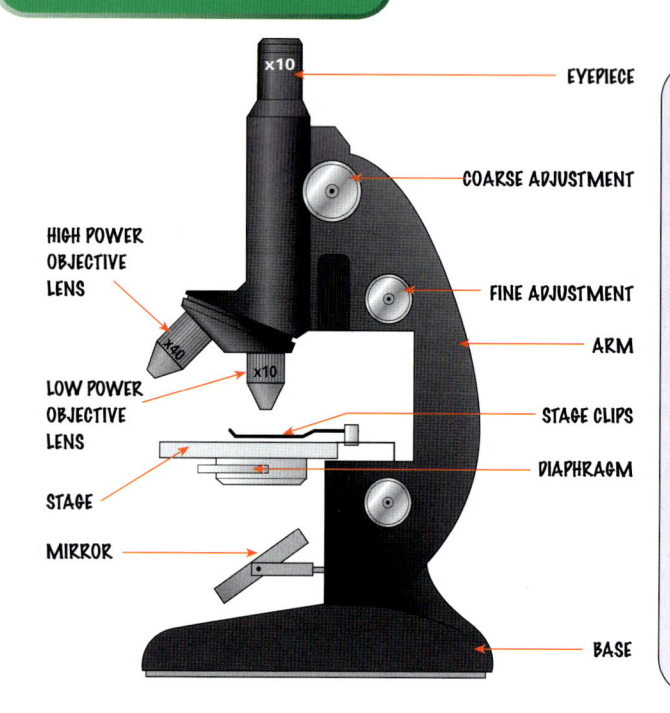

Labelled parts: EYEPIECE, COARSE ADJUSTMENT, HIGH POWER OBJECTIVE LENS, FINE ADJUSTMENT, ARM, LOW POWER OBJECTIVE LENS, STAGE CLIPS, DIAPHRAGM, STAGE, MIRROR, BASE

Follow these tips for successful viewing ...

1. Mount the object on a slide (see below)
2. Place the slide beneath the stage clips.
3. Place the low power OBJECTIVE LENS in position.
4. Open the diaphragm for maximum light.
5. Adjust the position of the mirror until you can clearly see light through the eye piece.
6. Focus by moving the low power objective lens away from the slide until the object is clear.
7. Close the diaphragm down a little if too much light is coming through the specimen.
8. Adjust the specimen so that it is in the centre of your field of view.

PREPARING A SLIDE

A good way to look at cells is to use onion epidermis ...
... which is that really thin (just one cell thick!) material between the layers of an onion.

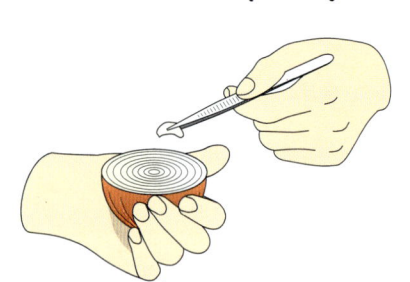

Peel a small strip of epidermis from a piece of onion.

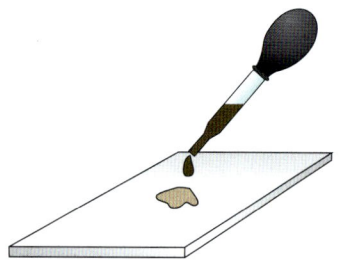

Add weak iodine solution to the specimen on a glass slide to stain it.

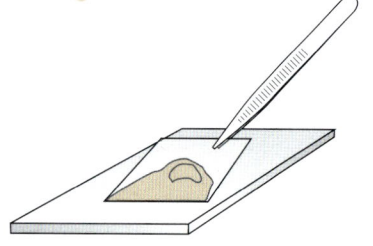

Carefully lower from one side a cover slip onto the sample. Take care to avoid air bubbles.

MAGNIFICATION

A microscope magnifies the object you are looking at.
The level of MAGNIFICATION is worked out by multiplying the 'power' of the EYEPIECE LENS by the 'power' of the objective lens.
For the microscope above it would be (x10) x (x10) = x 100 for the low power objective lens.

Lonsdale Science Revision Guides

THE STRUCTURE OF ANIMAL AND PLANT CELLS

Cells 2

CELL THEORY

The invention of the microscope led scientists to come up with a theory about living things ...
- All living things are made of cells.
- New cells are formed when old cells divide into 2 new cells.
- All cells are similar but not exactly the same.

If you look at onion epidermis under high power, you will see something very similar to the diagram in the top right hand corner of the page. These are plant cells which, if magnified further show features typical of plant cells.

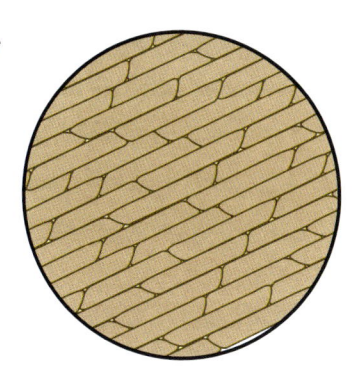

PLANT CELLS

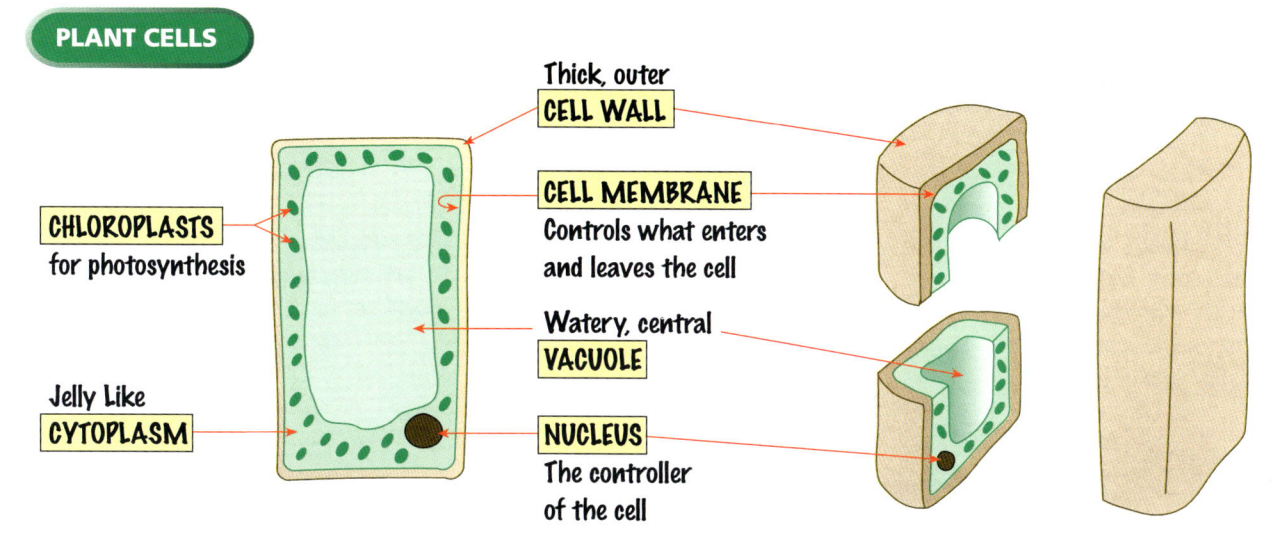

- Thick, outer **CELL WALL**
- **CELL MEMBRANE** Controls what enters and leaves the cell
- **CHLOROPLASTS** for photosynthesis
- Watery, central **VACUOLE**
- Jelly Like **CYTOPLASM**
- **NUCLEUS** The controller of the cell

Contrast the structures labelled here with the structures in a typical animal cell ...

ANIMAL CELLS

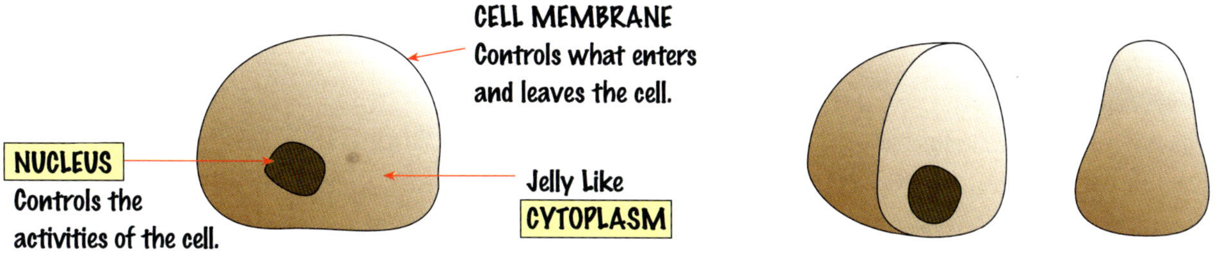

- **CELL MEMBRANE** Controls what enters and leaves the cell.
- **NUCLEUS** Controls the activities of the cell.
- Jelly Like **CYTOPLASM**

COMPARING PLANT AND ANIMAL CELLS

FEATURE	DESCRIPTION	PLANT CELLS	ANIMAL CELLS
NUCLEUS	Controls all the activities of the cell	YES	YES
CYTOPLASM	Chemical reactions happen in this jelly-like substance	YES	YES
CELL MEMBRANE	Controls what enters and leaves the cell	YES	YES
CELL WALL	Forms a rigid non-living box around the cell	YES	NO
VACUOLE	Large space containing cell sap (mainly water)	ALMOST ALWAYS	NO
CHLOROPLAST	The structures where photosynthesis happens	THOSE WHICH ARE EXPOSED TO LIGHT	NO

CELL SPECIALISATION AND THE ORGANISATION OF LIFE
● Cells 3

CELL SPECIALISATION

Cells often become adapted to perform different functions. We say they have become SPECIALISED to do a particular job. A specialised cell may develop a particular shape and may make different types of chemical substances in its cytoplasm. The human body has around 200 different types of cell, whereas plants have far fewer.

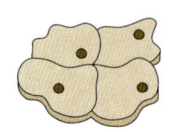

AN EPITHELIAL CELL
Covers large areas with a thin layer e.g. skin.

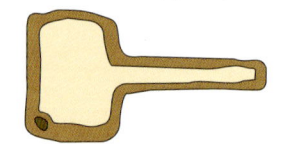

A ROOT HAIR CELL
The 'hair' helps to increase the surface area for absorption or water.

A NEURONE (OR NERVE CELL)
is long like a wire so that it can transmit 'messages'.

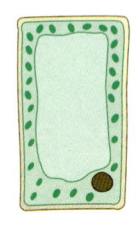

A PALISADE CELL
From the upper surface of a leaf. Packed with chloroplasts especially in the upper half to 'catch' lots of light.

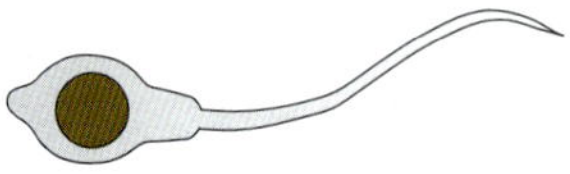

A SPERM CELL
Tiny but very mobile because of the tail.

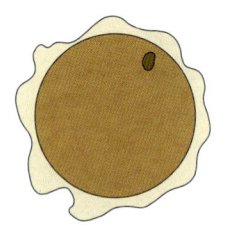

AN EGG CELL (OR OVUM)
Contains massive food resources for the developing embryo.

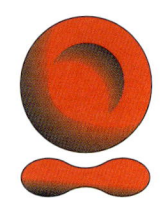

A RED BLOOD CELL
Loses its nucleus so that it can carry more oxygen around the human body.

A WHITE BLOOD CELL
can change its shape to engulf bacteria and then digest them.

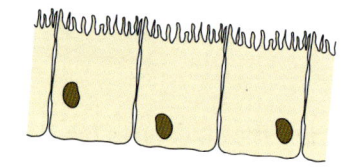

EPITHELIAL CELL
produce mucus and the cilia waft it towards the mouth and nose.

THE ORGANISATION OF LIFE

- Lots of cells with similar structure and function is called a TISSUE e.g. MUSCLE TISSUE, NERVOUS TISSUE.
- Two or more tissues working together is called an ORGAN e.g. BRAIN, KIDNEY, HEART, LUNG.

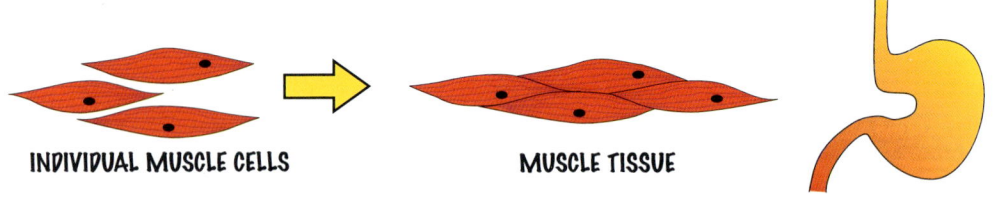

INDIVIDUAL MUSCLE CELLS → MUSCLE TISSUE

MUSCLE TISSUE COMBINES WITH OTHER TISSUES TO FORM AN ORGAN - E.G. THE STOMACH

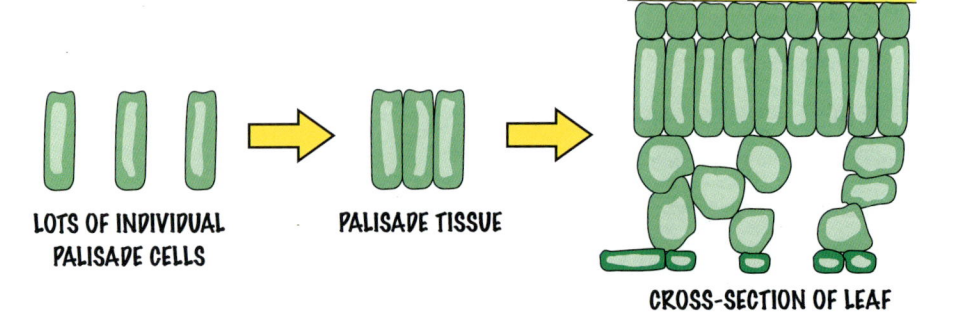

LOTS OF INDIVIDUAL PALISADE CELLS → PALISADE TISSUE → CROSS-SECTION OF LEAF

PALISADE TISSUE COMBINES WITH OTHER TISSUES TO FORM AN ORGAN - THE LEAF

CELL GROWTH AND REPRODUCTION
Cells — 4

CELL DIVISION AND GROWTH

Cells reproduce by DIVIDING, and then they grow to become as large as the original cell. The process is slightly different in animal and plant cells.

ANIMAL CELLS

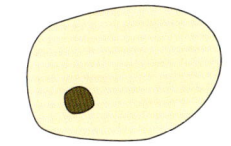

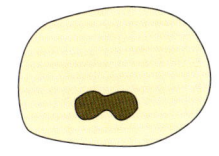

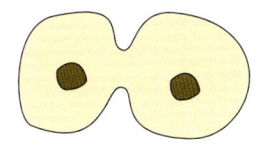

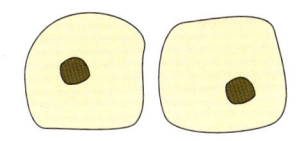

- First of all, the nucleus divides so that the new cells contain all the necessary information.
- The cytoplasm then divides to form two 'daughter' cells with a nucleus in each.

PLANT CELLS

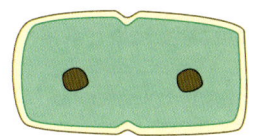

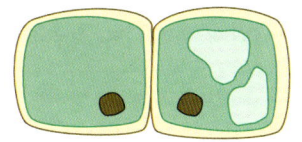

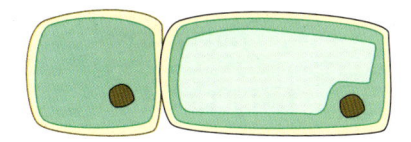

- Again, it's the nucleus which divides first for the same reasons as in animal cells.
- The cytoplasm now divides and the cell membrane forms between the TWO new cells.
- The vacuole starts to form and the cell furthest from the growing tip enlarges.
- The smallest cell (nearer the tip) will divide again and so on ...

THE GROWING TIPS OF PLANTS

- The cells at the tip are very small and constantly divide ...
  ... to make new cells.
- These new cells form vacuoles and increase in length ...
  ... as their distance from the growing tip increase.
- As they mature they specialise to form various plant tissues.

FERTILISATION IN FLOWERING PLANTS

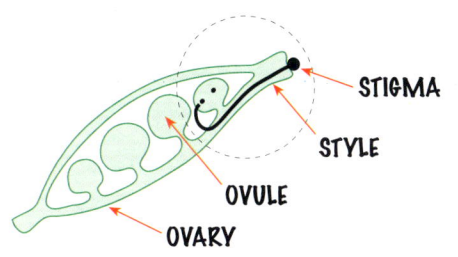

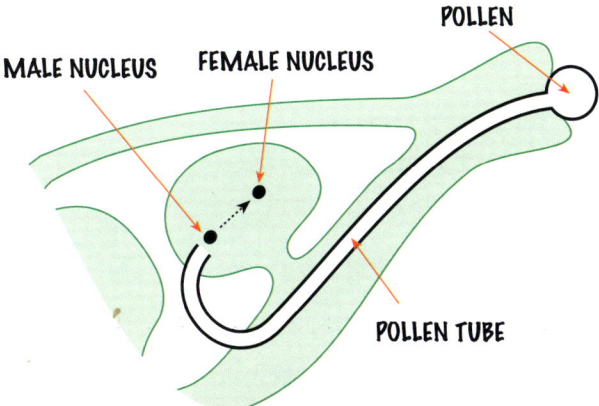

First of all, make sure you can remember the difference between **POLLINATION** and **FERTILISATION** ...

- Pollination is when pollen from the anthers is transferred to the stigma.
- If the pollen is from the same species of plant, ...
  ... a pollen tube starts to grow through the style, ...
  ... into the ovary and finally into an ovule.
- The pollen grain contains the male sex cell, and this travels down the pollen tube to fuse with the female sex cell which is inside the ovule. This is FERTILISATION.
- The male and female sex cells are specialised cells which enable information from two parent plants to be transferred to the next generation when the two sex cells fuse together.

Lonsdale Science Revision Guides

KEYWORDS AND COMPREHENSION — Cells 5

KEYWORDS

Match the keywords from this unit to their definitions ...

OBJECTIVE LENS	Controls all the activities of the cell and determines our characteristics
EYEPIECE LENS	The amount by which a microscope 'increases the size' of an object
MAGNIFICATION	The moment when the male and female sex cells fuse together
CELL WALL	The small green structures in plant cells in which photosynthesis occurs
CELL MEMBRANE	The microscope lens which is nearer to the object being viewed
VACUOLE	The microscope lens through which you look to view the object
NUCLEUS	When a cell has special features to help it to do its particular job
CYTOPLASM	When pollen from the anthers is transferred to the stigma
CHLOROPLASTS	Surrounds the cell and controls what enters and leaves it
SPECIALISED	A large space inside plant cells which contains cell sap (water mainly)
TISSUE	A rigid non-living box surrounding plant cells
ORGAN	This is a structure in which two or more tissues work together
POLLINATION	A jelly-like substance in the cell in which chemical reactions happen
FERTILISATION	This is made up of lots of cells with the same structure which do the same job

CELL THEORY

Read this passage and then answer the questions below ...

"The microscope, invented in the 17th Century, allowed Robert Hooke and others to observe structures as small as cells. Hooke used the word 'cell' to describe the dead cells he observed in 1665, but neither he nor anyone else realised that these 'empty cells' had once contained the basic units of life. Even when single celled animal life was observed in 1673 it was thought to have 'just formed' because no one had seen cell division. Improved microscopes in the 1830's allowed first, the discovery of the nucleus and secondly the discovery of cytoplasm. In 1839 Schwann and Schleiden suggested that cells were what organisms were made from and that organisms could be either single celled or multi celled. They recognised the membrane, nucleus and cytoplasm were common to all cells. In 1855, Virchow said that "all cells come from cells" and by 1890 all 'life' was thought to be made up of cells.

1. Why weren't cells recognised before the 17th Century?
2. When were the first living cells observed?
3. Why didn't the observer of these suggest that they were the 'unit of life'?
4. What was the single most important event in the discovery of the cell?
5. How did people explain the presence of cells before 'cell theory' became accepted.
6. What did Virchow mean by saying "all cells come from cells"?
7. Make a list showing the order in which these important discoveries were made and their dates.

TESTING UNDERSTANDING — Cells 6

MICROSCOPIC TROUBLE SHOOTING

If you can't view the specimen properly through your microscope you should check the following things ...

a) ... that the specimen is .... enough to allow light to pass through.

b) ... that the specimen is placed directly below the ....

c) ... that the .... has been 'Clicked' into the correct position.

d) ... that the .... is adjusted to allow the correct amount of light through.

e) ... that the specimen is in .... by adjusting the focusing knob.

f) ... that both the .... and .... are clean.

You must also remember to focus on the .... by moving the objective lens .... from the .... so that there is no danger of the two coming into contact. Always go through the checklist above before asking your teacher for help.

WHAT LIMITS CELL SIZE?

Oxygen and food can only pass into a cell through its surface. Imagine a perfectly cubic cell.

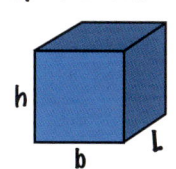

- Its surface area can be worked out by multiplying the area of one side by 6.
- Its volume can be worked out by multiplying length x breadth x height.

Complete the tables below and plot a line graph for each of them on the graph paper above

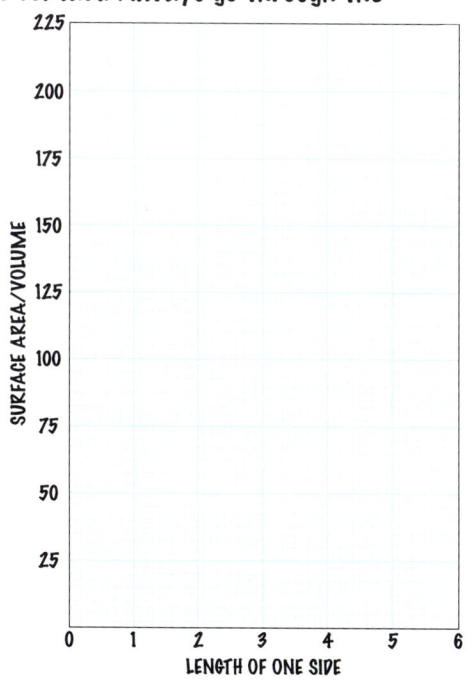

(Graph: SURFACE AREA/VOLUME vs LENGTH OF ONE SIDE, y-axis 0 to 225, x-axis 0 to 6)

LENGTH OF ONE SIDE	1	2	3	4	5	6
SURFACE AREA OF CELL h x b x 6	1 x 1 x 6 =	2 x 2 x 6 =	3 x 3 x 6 =	4 x 4 x 6 =	5 x 5 x 6 =	6 x 6 x 6 =

LENGTH OF ONE SIDE	1	2	3	4	5	6
VOLUME OF CELL L x b x h	1 x 1 x 1 =	2 x 2 x 2 =	3 x 3 x 3 =	4 x 4 x 4 =	5 x 5 x 5 =	6 x 6 x 6 =

Why don't cells grow as large as cricket balls?

....
....
....

Lonsdale Science Revision Guides

SCIENTIFIC INVESTIGATION

James and Yasmin were trying to decide which concentration of sugar solution is the best for germination of pollen grains.

They had 5 different solutions to use and were going to look at the pollen grains after a certain amount of time to see how many had germinated and produced a pollen tube.

- James decided to use 20 pollen grains in each sample.
- Yasmine decided to use 1 pollen grain in each sample.

1. What must be kept the same for this to be a fair test?

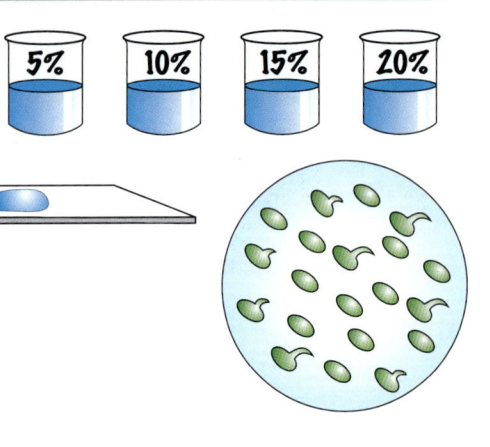

....

....

2. Which variable is being investigated here?

....

....

3. James's results were as follows ...

5% concentration made 7 germinate
0% concentration made 0 germinate
15% concentration made 5 germinate
20% concentration made 0 germinate
10% concentration made 13 germinate

Yasmine's results were as follows ...

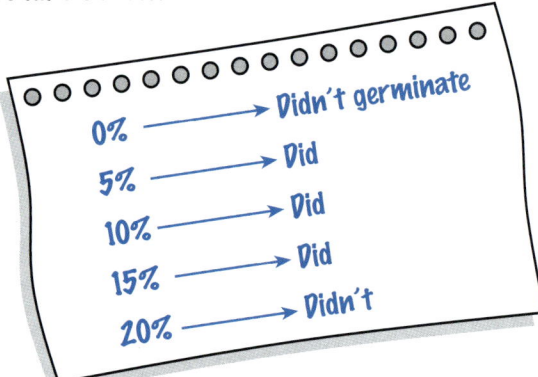

0% → Didn't germinate
5% → Did
10% → Did
15% → Did
20% → Didn't

4. Layout the best set of results in the table alongside and then plot them onto the graph paper. Make sure you produce the table in the correct order and don't forget to label the axes on the graph.

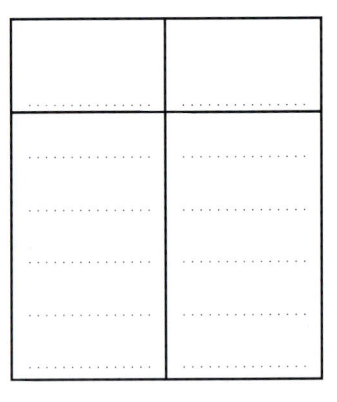

5. Which sugar concentration is the best for germination of pollen grains? ....

6. Why is it important to have a big enough sample size in this type of investigation?

....

....

PATTERNS OF SEXUAL REPRODUCTION

Reproduction — 1

TYPES OF FERTILISATION

Fertilisation happens when a sperm meets an egg, and is the moment when a new life begins. There are TWO types ...

EXTERNAL FERTILISATION
This takes place outside the bodies of the parents.

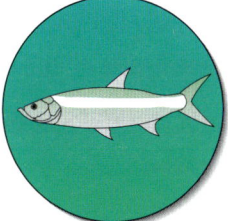

- Fish can release sperm and eggs as they swim along side each other, but some build simple "nests" into which the eggs are first laid e.g. Sticklebacks.
- In frogs, the male clings to the female and they release sperm and eggs at the same time.

INTERNAL FERTILISATION
This takes place inside the body of the female.

- Sperm is released directly into the female's body ... ... where it must swim to the egg.
- Reptiles and birds produce their eggs after fertilisation.
- These all produce less offspring, even reptiles which can still produce lots!

KEY DIFFERENCES BETWEEN EXTERNAL AND INTERNAL FERTILISATION

EXTERNAL	INTERNAL
Lots of eggs produced (between thousands and millions).	Far fewer eggs produced (between one and several hundred).
Many eggs remain unfertilised.	Most eggs are fertilised.
Parent's job is done after fertilisation.	To some extent the parent (female) is still responsible.
Smaller percentage of offspring survive to maturity.	Greater proportion of offspring survive to maturity.
Offspring very immature when they hatch.	Offspring more mature when they hatch.

PARENTAL RESPONSIBILITY

- In external fertilisation there is no parental responsibility since the fertilised eggs are just left alone with the result that the vast majority are eaten.
- Internal fertilisation in egg layers at least involves the laying of eggs in some sort of nest and in the case of birds the eggs have to be kept warm. In mammals, the young actually develop to a certain extent inside the body of the female before they are born. Together with the milk provided by the mother, this level of aftercare gives an increased chance of survival by producing a more 'mature' youngster who has access to a constant supply of food.

THE MECHANISM OF HUMAN REPRODUCTION — Reproduction 2

THE SEX CELLS

There are TWO types, the female cell or egg and the male cell or sperm. These cells are specially adapted to their function.

- The sperm has a tail to 'push' it along ...

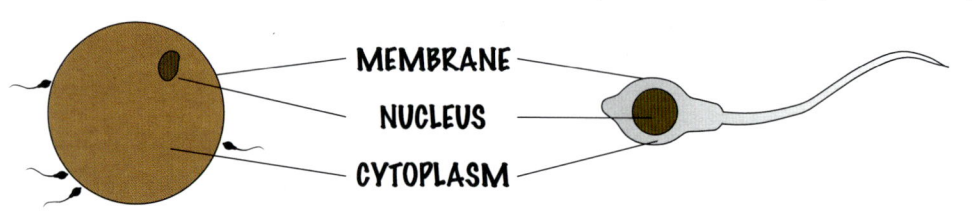

MEMBRANE
NUCLEUS
CYTOPLASM

- The egg is an enlarged cell with massive food reserves.

- ... a specially designed head to help it to break through the membrane of the egg ...

- ... and a streamlined shape because it has very little cytoplasm.

When a sperm enters an egg, its nucleus fuses with the egg cell nucleus. This combines the inherited information from the mother and the father to form a new individual who has characteristics of both parents. The newly fertilised egg now starts to divide.

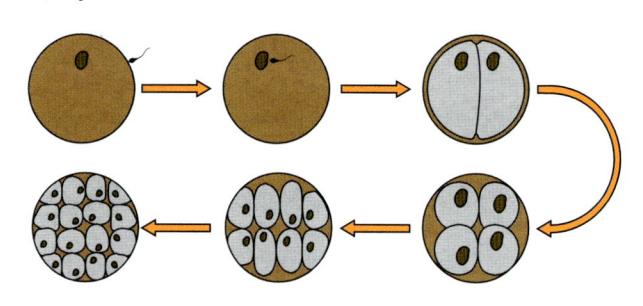

THE MALE AND FEMALE REPRODUCTIVE SYSTEMS

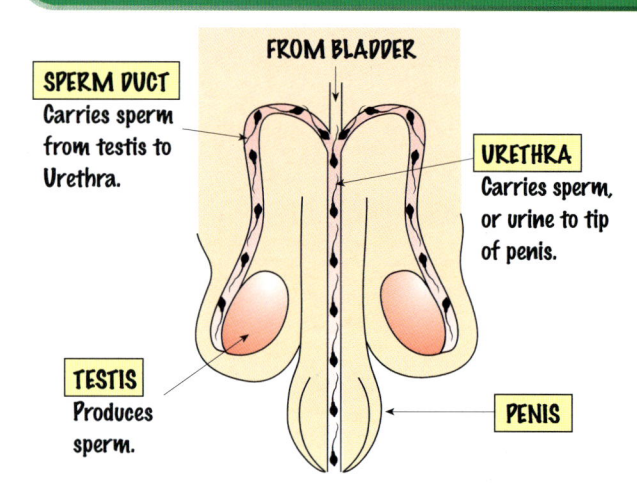

FROM BLADDER

SPERM DUCT Carries sperm from testis to Urethra.

URETHRA Carries sperm, or urine to tip of penis.

TESTIS Produces sperm.

PENIS

- Sperm is continually produced in the TESTES.
- When sexually aroused the penis becomes erect and may be inserted into the vagina.
- Sperms may then be ejaculated at the neck of the uterus (the cervix). This means they are squeezed along the sperm ducts and out of the tip of the penis.

- From the cervix, the sperm will swim through the uterus and up into the oviducts.
- Here, it may meet and fuse with ...
  ... an egg cell which will have been released within the past two days or so by one of the ovaries.
- Unfertilised egg cells only last for a maximum of 3 days - whereas sperm may survive for longer.

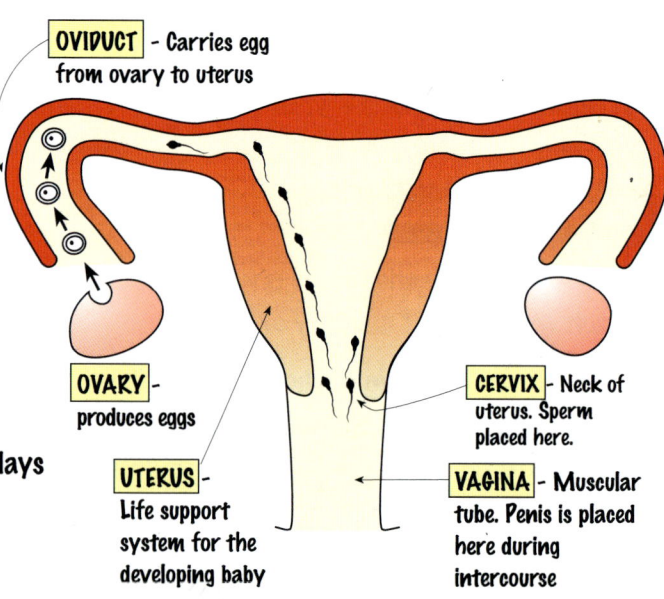

OVIDUCT - Carries egg from ovary to uterus

OVARY - produces eggs

UTERUS - Life support system for the developing baby

CERVIX - Neck of uterus. Sperm placed here.

VAGINA - Muscular tube. Penis is placed here during intercourse

THE MENSTRUAL CYCLE AND FOETAL DEVELOPMENT — Reproduction 3

THE MENSTRUAL CYCLE

A sexually mature female releases an egg every month from one of her ovaries. Her uterus lining must prepare itself to receive this egg in the event that it is fertilised. The MENSTRUAL CYCLE looks like this:

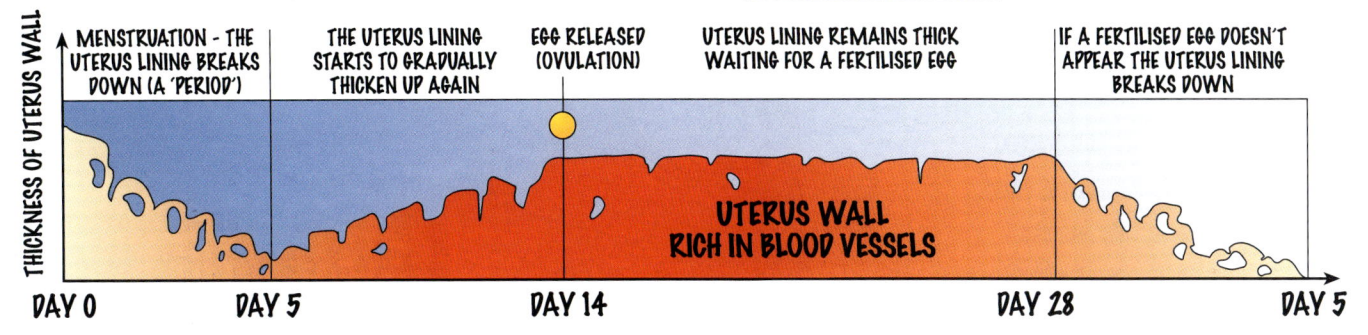

DAY 0	DAY 5	DAY 14	DAY 28	DAY 5
MENSTRUATION - THE UTERUS LINING BREAKS DOWN (A 'PERIOD')	THE UTERUS LINING STARTS TO GRADUALLY THICKEN UP AGAIN	EGG RELEASED (OVULATION)	UTERUS LINING REMAINS THICK WAITING FOR A FERTILISED EGG	IF A FERTILISED EGG DOESN'T APPEAR THE UTERUS LINING BREAKS DOWN

(Y-axis: THICKNESS OF UTERUS WALL. UTERUS WALL RICH IN BLOOD VESSELS)

It is important to realise that this is an example and in reality all women are different.

FERTILISATION

For fertilisation to have the best chance of happening, sperm must be in the oviduct at the same time that the egg is there. So, in the diagram above, sexual intercourse between days 12 - 15 could result in the following sequence ...

1. **OVULATION** (release of egg from ovary).
   (INTERCOURSE - sperm ejaculated into vagina).
2. **FERTILISATION** (fusion of sperm and egg).
3. **CELL DIVISION** (to form ball of cells, then embryo).
4. **IMPLANTATION** (into spongy lining of uterus).

DEVELOPMENT OF THE FOETUS

After about 9 or 10 weeks the limbs are visible and the EMBRYO becomes a FOETUS. The PLACENTA plays an important role during development ...

1. It brings the FOETAL blood into close contact with the mother's blood so that ...
   ... OXYGEN, WATER + FOOD pass into the foetal blood ...
   ... and CARBON DIOXIDE + WASTE pass into mum's blood.

   NB. THE TWO BLOOD SUPPLIES DO NOT MIX.

2. It acts as a BARRIER to <u>some</u> harmful substances. But unfortunately some substances and viruses can cross the placenta and harm the child e.g. Rubella (German measles), many drugs, alcohol and substances in cigarette smoke.

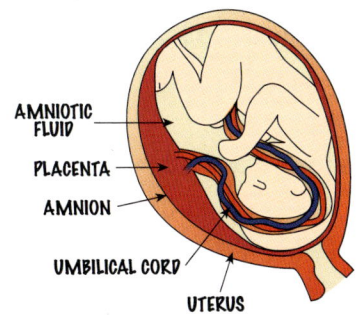

PROTECTION INSIDE THE UTERUS

- Inside the uterus the baby lives in a membranous sac called the amnion ...
- ... filled with AMNIOTIC FLUID (the 'waters').
- This acts as a kind of 'shock absorber' ...
- ... to support the baby and protect it from minor bumps.

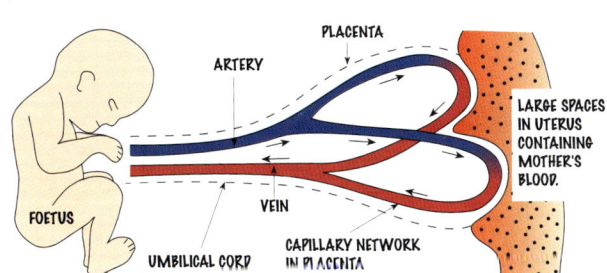

BIRTH ONWARDS

● Reproduction 4

BIRTH

PLACENTA - which is implanted in the wall of the uterus.

UMBILICAL CORD - attaches the baby to the placenta.

BABY INSIDE THE AMNION - surrounded by amniotic fluid. The bag eventually bursts (breaking of the waters).

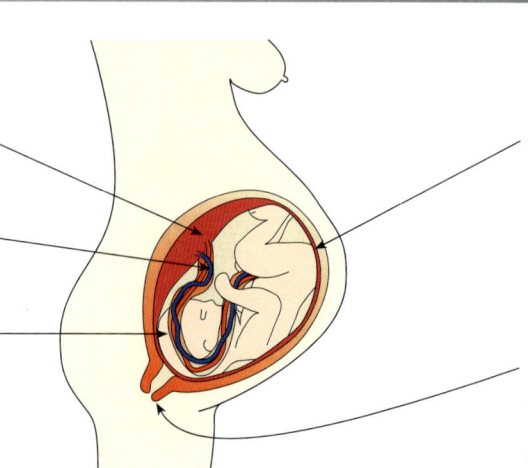

The muscles in the uterus wall contract strongly ('contractions') in order to push the baby out, followed by the placenta.

The muscles in the cervix ('neck of the womb') relax and widen to allow the baby to leave the uterus.

MILK PRODUCTION

The newborn baby will respond by turning its head when its cheek is touched and by sucking when a nipple is placed in its mouth. These are reflex (automatic) actions, and sucking on the nipple causes the production of more milk in its mother's mammary glands (breasts). This milk is highly nutritious and also provides some protection from infection.

HUMAN LIFE CYCLE

After birth, a child grows to adulthood. The growth rate is mainly steady but also has some remarkable spurts at various times (my word, he's shot up!).
Rapid cell division followed by cell growth accounts for the increase in size.

ADOLESCENCE

This is the time when a human's reproductive organs become mature, and physically the person changes from a boy or girl into an adult.

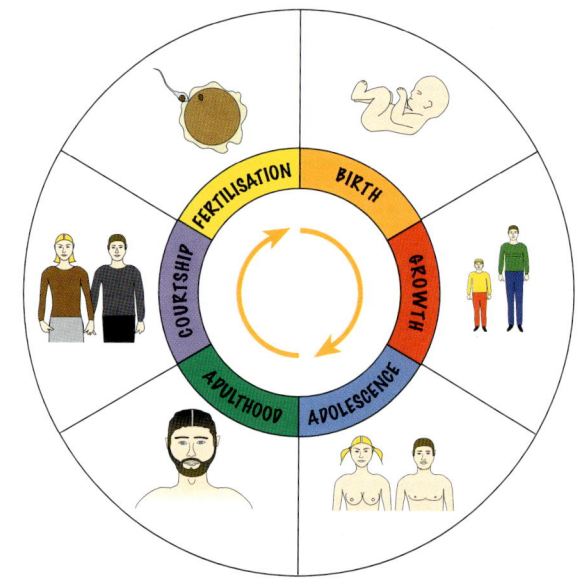

PHYSICAL CHANGES WHICH TAKE PLACE DURING ADOLESCENCE

GIRLS	BOYS
• OVARIES START TO RELEASE EGGS • BREASTS START TO DEVELOP • HIPS GET BROADER • PUBIC AND UNDER ARM HAIR GROWS • STRONGER BODY SMELL	• TESTES START TO PRODUCE SPERM • MUSCLES AND PENIS GROW BIGGER • VOICE BECOMES DEEPER • PUBIC, FACIAL AND UNDERARM HAIR GROWS • STRONGER BODY SMELL

These physical changes are also accompanied by EMOTIONAL CHANGES, caused by changing levels of hormones in the body. These may include ...
- ... interest in the opposite sex, • ... irritability, • ... mood swings, • ... embarrassment.
   At this time there is often friction with parents due mainly to the fact that although a person may physically be mature they are still emotionally immature.
- Unfortunately the adolescent tends not to realise this at the time! We all usually get through it O.K. in the end though.

KEYWORDS AND COMPREHENSION
Reproduction — 5

KEYWORDS

Match the keywords from this unit to their definitions ...

SPERM DUCT	Carries sperm or urine to the tip of the penis
TESTIS	One of two organs which produce eggs
URETHRA	A life support system for the developing baby
OVIDUCT	The monthly series of changes in the female reproduction system
OVARY	One of two organs which produce sperm
UTERUS	The monthly release of an egg from one of the ovaries
VAGINA	The name given to the developing baby for the first 9 or 10 weeks
MENSTRUAL CYCLE	Carries sperm from the testis to the urethra
OVULATION	The 'waters' which protect the baby from minor bumps
IMPLANTATION	Carries the eggs from the ovary to the uterus
EMBRYO	The organ connecting the embryo to the uterus
PLACENTA	When the fertilised egg attaches itself to the lining of the uterus
AMNIOTIC FLUID	The fusing together of an egg and a sperm
FERTILISATION	Muscular tube where the penis is placed during intercourse

MULTIPLE BIRTHS

Read the passage below and answer the questions below.

Sometimes a pregnant woman gives birth to two or more children which we call twins, triplets or quads etc. These children may be identical or non-identical. Identical twins are caused when an egg is fertilised and begins to divide to form the ball of cells. This ball of cells suddenly splits into two groups of cells and each of them implants into the wall of the uterus and develops into separate but identical individuals. Non-identical twins are formed when the ovary release two eggs at the same time which are fertilised by two different sperms. These implant in the same way as identical twins but are genetically different individuals.

1. How many sperms are needed to produced identical twins? Explain your answer.
2. How many sperms are needed to produce non-identical twins? Explain your answer.
3. How many eggs are needed to produce identical twins? Explain your answer.
4. How many eggs are needed to produce non-identical twins? Explain your answer.
5. What would happen if two eggs were released from an ovary at the same time but only one was fertilised?
6. What would the result be if two eggs were released at the same time and both were fertilised, but before implantation one of them divided into two?
7. What risks could be associated with a multiple pregnancy?

TESTING UNDERSTANDING

Reproduction 6

THE SEQUENCE OF EVENTS

Each month, one of the female's .... releases an .... This then travels down one of the .... towards the .... The walls of the .... have gradually thickened during the previous .... days as they get ready to receive a fertilised egg. If sexual intercourse has taken place at the right time, the .... may meet with a .... and .... may take place. If this happens, ... takes place rapidly so that by the time the .... is reached, the single cell has formed a .... which may .... in the thick spongy wall. This new life is called an .... until about 9 or 10 weeks after which it is called a .... The developing baby remains inside its mother for approximately 40 weeks protected by the .... fluid. After this time the baby is born and is fed on .... produced by its mother's ....

A GROWING PROBLEM

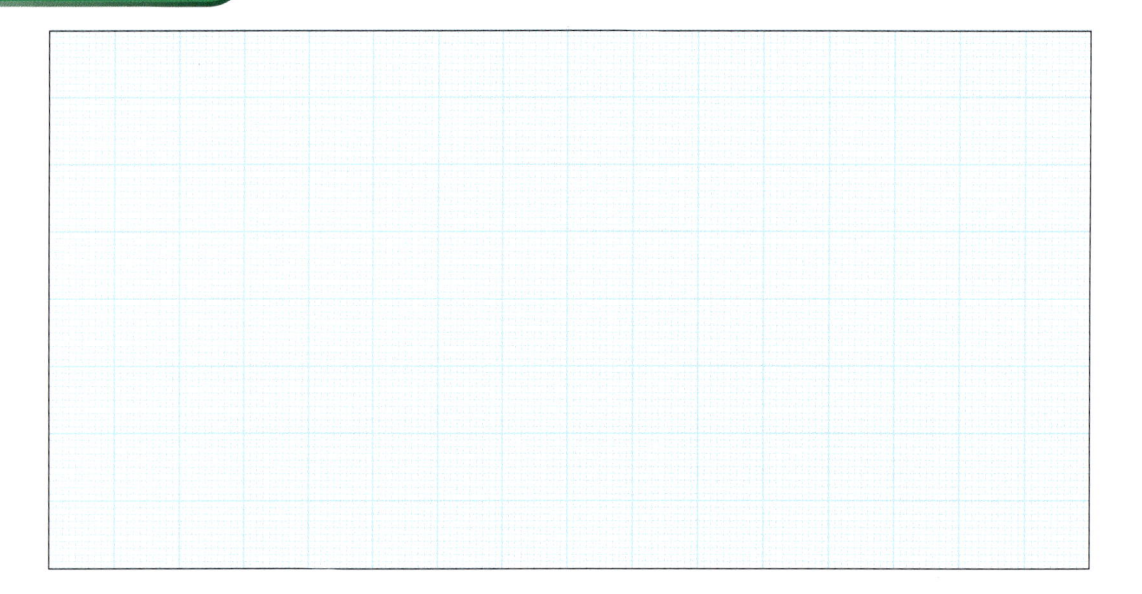

Plot the data below onto the graph paper as two separate line graphs.

AGE (YEARS)	BIRTH	2	4	6	8	10	12	14	16
GRACE'S HEIGHT (cm)	37	86	98	114	138	142	156	174	186
CHRIS' HEIGHT (cm)	34	90	105	121	141	152	163	179	191

SCIENTIFIC INVESTIGATION

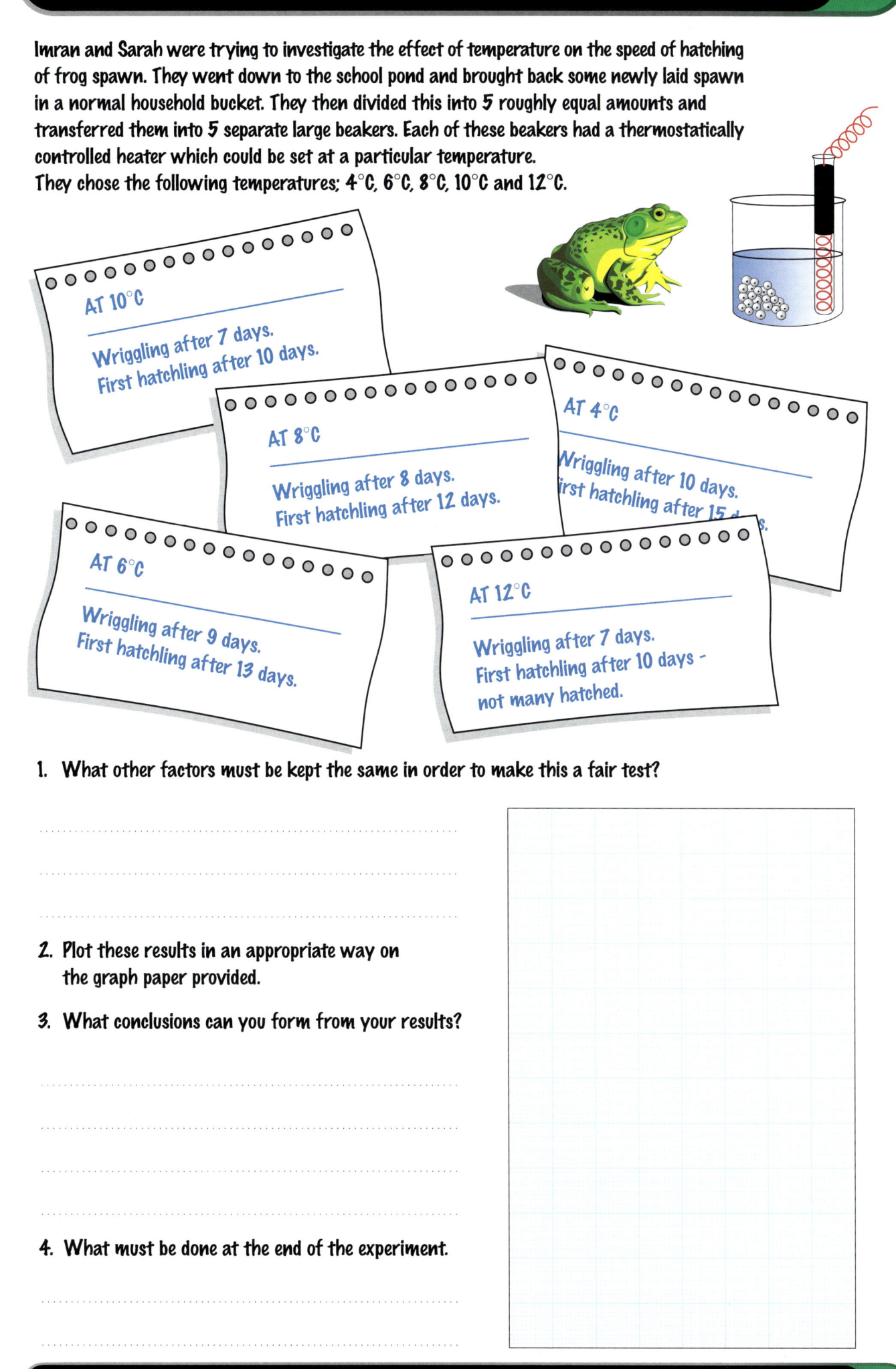

Reproduction — 7

Imran and Sarah were trying to investigate the effect of temperature on the speed of hatching of frog spawn. They went down to the school pond and brought back some newly laid spawn in a normal household bucket. They then divided this into 5 roughly equal amounts and transferred them into 5 separate large beakers. Each of these beakers had a thermostatically controlled heater which could be set at a particular temperature.
They chose the following temperatures; 4°C, 6°C, 8°C, 10°C and 12°C.

AT 10°C
Wriggling after 7 days.
First hatchling after 10 days.

AT 8°C
Wriggling after 8 days.
First hatchling after 12 days.

AT 4°C
Wriggling after 10 days.
First hatchling after 15 days.

AT 6°C
Wriggling after 9 days.
First hatchling after 13 days.

AT 12°C
Wriggling after 7 days.
First hatchling after 10 days – not many hatched.

1. What other factors must be kept the same in order to make this a fair test?

2. Plot these results in an appropriate way on the graph paper provided.

3. What conclusions can you form from your results?

4. What must be done at the end of the experiment.

Lonsdale Science Revision Guides

ADAPTATION TO HABITAT

Environment and Feeding Relationships — 1

HABITATS

'A habitat is the particular type of area in which an animal or plant lives.'

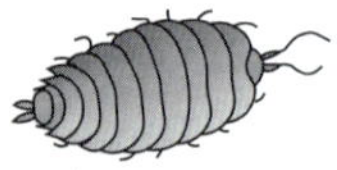

e.g. Woodlice live in dark damp areas beneath rotting material.

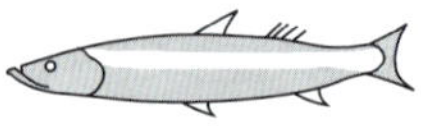

e.g. Sticklebacks live among weeds in ponds.

e.g. Mussels live around the low tide mark on rocky beaches.

e.g. Slugs live in gaps and cracks in stone walls.

The following are some of the features which vary from one habitat to another ...

... LIGHT    ... TEMPERATURE    ... OXYGEN 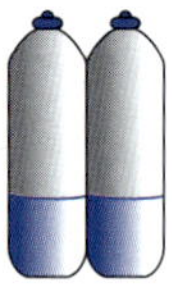   ... WATER    ... NUTRIENTS

Because of these variations in conditions, animals and plants are found in habitats to which they are well suited. We say they are adapted to their habitat.

EXAMPLES OF ADAPTATIONS TO DIFFERENT HABITATS

THE COLD OF THE ARCTIC
- Thick layer of fat for storage and INSULATION.
- Thick, waterproof fur for insulation.
- Large feet to distribute weight over snow and ice.
- White colour for camouflage.
- HIBERNATION in worst weather.

THE DRYNESS OF THE DESERT
- Leaves are reduced to spines to reduce water loss ... 
   ... and to keep grazing animals away.
- Swollen stem stores water.
- Widespreading roots to absorb water quickly.

THE CHANGING TIDES
- The ability to hold fast to rocks or even other mussels prevents them from being washed away.
- During low tide they close shut completely to avoid drying out.

THE DEMANDS OF WATER
- A streamlined shape allows them to 'cut through' the water. 
- Fins allow great manoeuvrability.
- Gills allow the fish to take in oxygen which is dissolved in the water.

BURROWING UNDERGROUND
- A streamlined shape makes burrowing easier.
- Large powerful front paws for digging.
- Poor sight but great sense of smell and awareness of vibration.

THE SHADE OF THE WOODLAND
- Bluebells and other woodland plants tend to have an early growing season and are early flowering to make the most of the light before the canopy of trees develops.
- Some plants climb on other trees to get light.

WHY ADAPTATIONS ARE SO IMPORTANT

ADAPTATIONS are special features or behaviour which make an organism especially well-suited to its environment, and therefore increase its chances of survival.
- All living organisms are adapted to the natural habitat in which they live ...
- ... their adaptations make them successful in that particular environment.

ADAPTATIONS TO DAILY AND SEASONAL CHANGE

Environment and Feeding Relationships — 2

ADAPTATION TO DAILY CHANGES

The physical environment around your school varies dramatically over any 24hr period. Things which change include: LIGHT INTENSITY, TEMPERATURE, HUMIDITY AND NOISE LEVEL ...

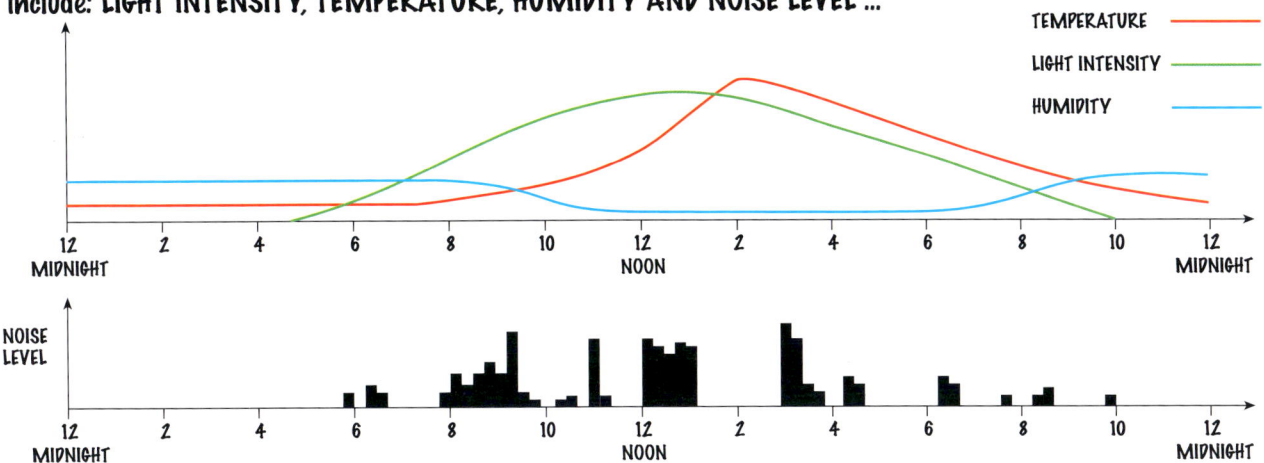

For a typical school on a typical day these 4 factors may vary according to the graphs above. These changes could be responsible for behavioural changes in the animal population, and could result in different animals visiting the school at different times e.g. ...

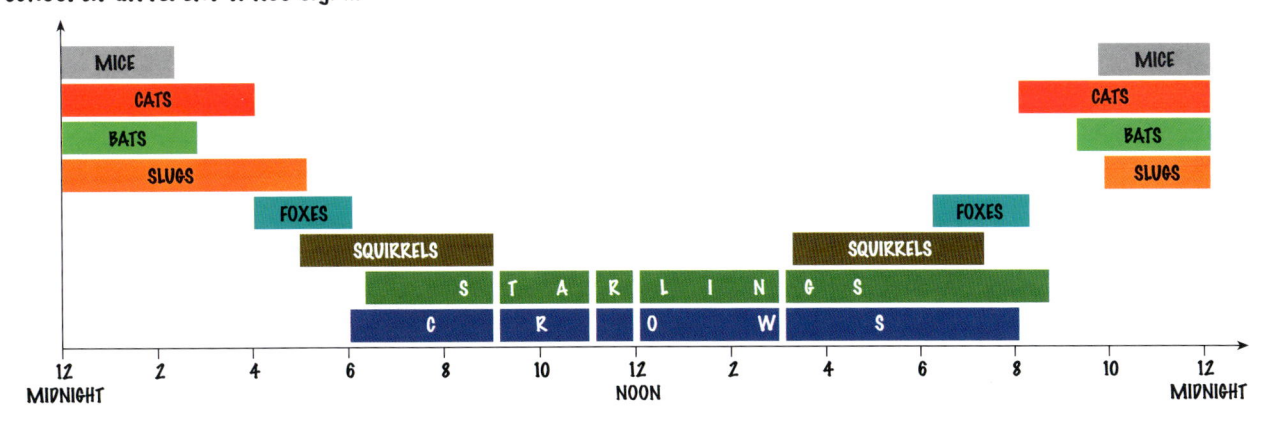

ADAPTATION TO SEASONAL CHANGES

Although seasonal changes tend to occur more gradually, their effects tend to be greater than daily changes and result in animals and plants having to develop strategies (plans) to avoid suffering climatic stress. e.g. ...

1. **HIBERNATION** - Some animals build up a fat layer and sleep through the worst winter months.

2. **MIGRATION** - Animals move off to warmer climates. This is a good move but needs a lot of energy.

3. **INSULATION** - Many animals grow thicker fur, in some cases white to give them the extra advantage of camouflage.

4. LEAF SHEDDING - not much light in winter and the ground water's probably frozen so no point in losing water through leaves you aren't using?

5. RETREATING UNDERGROUND - perennial plants die back and 'live' underground on stored food reserves. e.g. potatoes

6. FOOD STORING - squirrels are pretty good at this. e.g. hazelnuts

7. OVERWINTERING of PUPAE - Many insects have a life cycle in which there is a dormant ("sleeping") phase which helps them to survive the winter.

Lonsdale Science Revision Guides

FEEDING RELATIONSHIPS

Environment and Feeding Relationships — 3

FOOD CHAINS

These show us the different feeding relationships in a certain area. In other words "what's eating what?" They show that energy from the sun is 'trapped' by green plants which then pass energy on to the animals which eat them.

Sun → ENERGY → cabbage/carrots → ENERGY → rabbit → ENERGY → fox

Sun → ENERGY → wheat → ENERGY → mice → ENERGY → stoat

- The green plants are called the **PRODUCERS** because they produce the energy for the food chain.
- The animals in the chain are called the **CONSUMERS** i.e. they eat things to get their energy.
- Plant eating animals are called **HERBIVORES.** Animal eating animals are called **CARNIVORES.**
- Animals which eat both animals and plants are called **OMNIVORES.**

PREDATORS AND THEIR PREY

If one animal eats another, then the animal doing the eating is the **PREDATOR,** and the animal being eaten is the **PREY.** In the food chains above, the fox and stoat are predators and the rabbit and fieldmouse are their prey.

Predators show adaptations for finding, catching and killing their prey ...

- Predator's eyes point directly forwards to give them good judgement of distance. Their eyesight is very acute.
- They hunt by stealth, often ambushing their prey. 
- They often have an excellent sense of smell.
- They may have sharp claws (talons), and sharp beaks or teeth.
- They are often well camouflaged, or good at keeping out of sight.

Prey Species also show adaptations to avoid being found, caught and killed ...

- Most have eyes at the sides of their heads to give them close to full all round vision. They are very alert and easily startled.
- They may crowd together in groups. 
- They often have acute hearing and a good sense of smell.
- They may have armour or spines to put predators off.
- They are often well camouflaged, and many are nocturnal.

FOOD WEBS AND COMPETITION BETWEEN ANIMALS
Environment and Feeding Relationships • 4

FOOD WEBS

Food chains connect together to form food webs which show the feeding relationship in a particular environment i.e. who's eating whom!

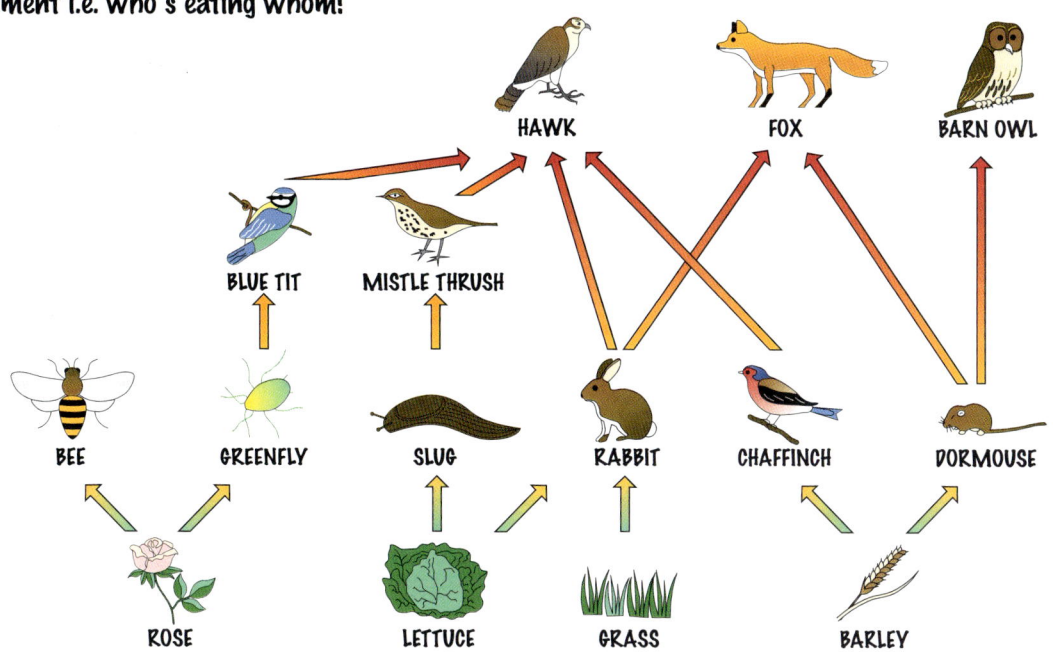

COMPETITION

In the food web above there are lots of food chains interlinking with each other. This means that various animals are in competition with other species for their food source. In this food web, the fox is in competition with the hawk for rabbits, but the rabbit is in competition with the slugs for lettuce!

The lettuce may have to compete for light, space and water with other plants but has little or no defence against the slugs and rabbits, unlike plants such as holly or nettles which have spines and stings to defend them.

BREAKING THE LINKS

Because everything in the food web is so interdependent, ...
... if one species dies off then many others can be affected. For instance, if all the rabbits died in the food web above ...

- ... the lettuces and the grass could start to do well,
- ... but the hawks and foxes may reduce in number due to lack of food, unless ... they started eating more blue tits, thrushes and chaffinches in the case of the hawk, or more dormice in the case of the foxes.
- Also the increase in lettuces may cause a big increase in slugs and therefore thrushes.

ADDING NEW LINKS

If new species arrive on the scene then the whole food web will be forced to change to accommodate them. For instance if some stoats appeared, they would compete for rabbits, dormice and slugs. This would put these populations under more pressure and their numbers would go down. The hawk, fox and barn owl may also suffer due to lack of food.

KEYWORDS AND COMPREHENSION
Environment and Feeding Relationships — 5

KEYWORDS

Match the keywords from this unit to their definitions ...

HABITAT	Sleeping through the coldest periods of the year
ADAPTATION	Growing thicker fur or putting on extra fat beneath the skin
HIBERNATION	All animals since they have to eat things for their energy
MIGRATION	Animals which eat only other animals
INSULATION	An animal which hunts other animals
PRODUCER	A sequence of organisms showing energy transfer between them
CONSUMER	Lots of inter-connected food chains
HERBIVORE	The particular type of area in which an animal or plant lives
CARNIVORE	An animal which is hunted by other animals
OMNIVORE	Moving to a warmer place to avoid the worst of the winter
PREDATOR	Animals which eat only plants
PREY	Characteristics which make an organism well suited to its environment
FOOD WEB	Animals which eat both plants and other animals
FOOD CHAIN	A green plant because it produces the food for the food chain

WHO'S EATING WHAT

Read this passage and then answer the questions below.

Investigation of a local lake revealed the following food web. The green plants were Canadian pond weed, water lily, **and** algae **and these were fed on by** insect larvae, small crustaceans **and** tadpoles. **In turn, the** small crustaceans **and** insect larvae **were fed on by** roach, water beetles **and** frogs, **while the** tadpoles **were eaten only by** waterbeetles. **The** roach **and** frogs **were eaten by** perch **and** pike **but the** waterbeetles **were only eaten by** perch. Perch **were also eaten by** pike.

1. Which organisms are producers?
2. Which organisms are herbivores?
3. Which organisms are carnivores?
4. Write down a food chain containing 5 organisms which doesn't include frogs or waterbeetles?
5. If all the water beetles died or were removed, which organism would benefit the most?
6. If all the tadpoles died or were removed, which organism would suffer the most?
7. Which organisms would be most affected by the death or removal of all the perch?
   Explain your answer fully.

22 — *Lonsdale* Science Revision Guides

TESTING UNDERSTANDING

Environment and Feeding Relationships — 6

ADAPT OR DIE

Adaptations are characteristics which increase an organism's chances of .... All organisms are adapted to their .... Animals which live in water all the time tend to have a .... shape. Animals which live underground in burrows tend to have poor .... but a good sense of .... Animals which fly usually have light .... and specially shaped .... which provide lift. Some animals change to suit the particular season by shedding or growing .... , or putting on or losing .... beneath the skin. Animals which hunt and capture other animals are called .... and have features to help them do this. These may include sharp .... and .... Also they may be .... so that they can creep up on animals without being noticed. Animals which are caught and eaten are called .... , and their adaptations may also include good .... so that they aren't noticed, and good senses of .... and .... Their eyes are often on the side of their head whereas a .... point directly forward.

PREDATOR PREY RELATIONSHIPS

Ladybirds are predators of greenfly. The figures show how the numbers of greenfly and ladybirds change over 3 years.

TIME	No. OF LADYBIRDS (000's)	No. OF GREENFLY (000's)
JAN 97	5	10
APR 97	25	80
JUL 97	45	100
OCT 97	60	30
JAN 98	30	20
APR 98	10	70
JUL 98	35	110
OCT 98	75	50
JAN 99	20	30
APR 99	35	50
JULY 99	60	80
OCT 99	75	30

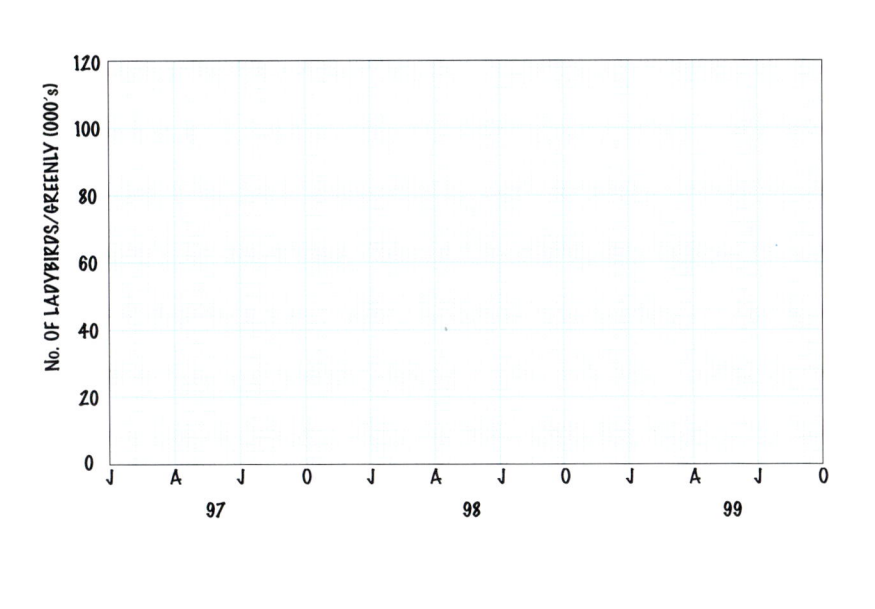

Plot these results onto the graph paper provided and explain what's happening.

SCIENTIFIC INVESTIGATION

Environment and Feeding Relationships — 7

Several students carried out an investigation into the sort of conditions that woodlice prefer. They used a 'choice chamber' to perform this task. The chamber is divided into light and dark halves, and wet and dry halves. This provides 4 choices for the woodlice, wet and dark, wet and light, dry and dark, dry and light.

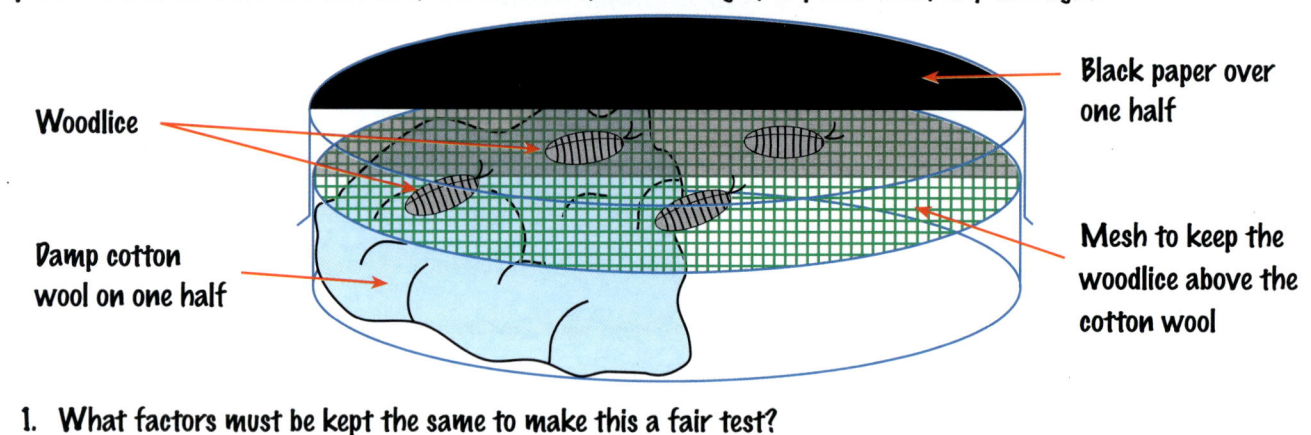

- Woodlice
- Damp cotton wool on one half
- Black paper over one half
- Mesh to keep the woodlice above the cotton wool

1. What factors must be kept the same to make this a fair test?

2. The students recorded where the woodlice were, every 2 minutes.

TIME	0	2	4	6	8	10
Wet + Dark	5	11	16	18	19	20
Wet + Light	5	3	1	0	0	0
Dry + Dark	5	4	3	2	1	0
Dry + Light	5	2	0	0	0	0

Plot these results on the graph below using a different colour for each set of conditions.

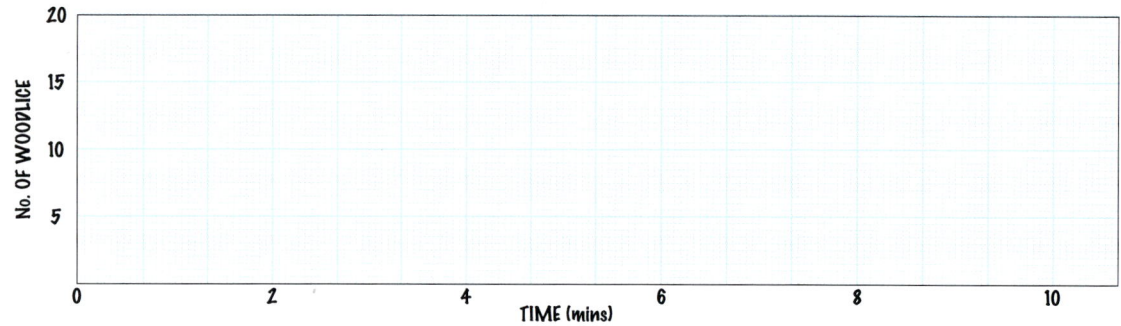

3. What conclusions can you draw from this investigation?

4. If the experiment had been done with only 4 woodlice, would the results have been as useful? Explain your answer?

5. What sort of conditions do woodlice least like?

VARIATION IN INDIVIDUALS

Variation and Classification — 1

EXAMPLES OF VARIATION

Differences between organisms of the same species is called **VARIATION.**

WEIGHT   INTELLIGENCE
HEIGHT   EYE COLOUR
HAIR COLOUR   LEFT/RIGHT HANDEDNESS
HAND WIDTH   SKIN COLOUR
ARM LENGTH   SHOE SIZE

Here are two examples for you to measure amongst your class mates ...

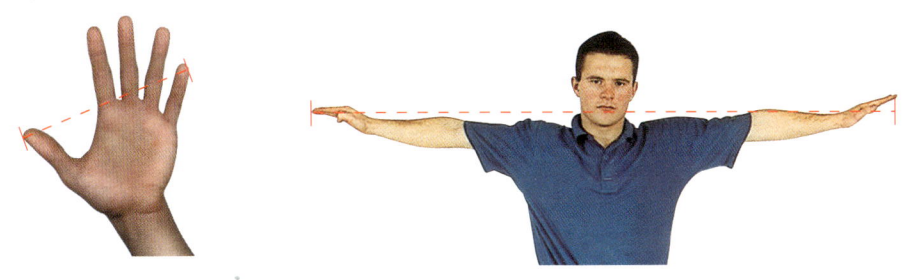

USING DATA ON VARIATION

Whatever you decide to investigate you must produce a table to display your results.
This usually describes the category and the number of people who fit into this particular category ...

HEIGHT (cm)	No. OF PUPILS
151-155	2
156-160	5
161-165	8

These can be used to produce graphs which give you a better 'picture' of your results.
This particular data may produce a graph which looks something like the one in fig.1 below.
If we took the same data from a Yr.9 class we might get something like the one in Fig.2 as the pupils are generally taller.

FIG 1. HEIGHT OF PUPILS IN YEAR 7 CLASS

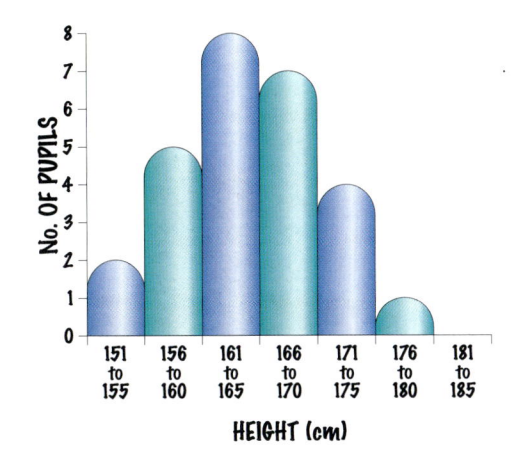

FIG 2. HEIGHT OF PUPILS IN YEAR 9 CLASS

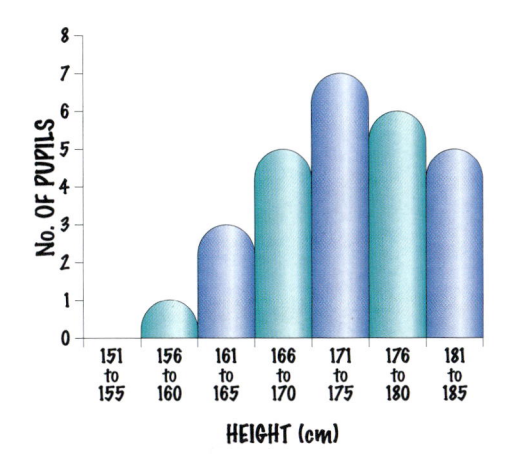

CAUSES OF VARIATION

Variation and Classification 2

INHERITANCE v ENVIRONMENT

What you are depends on the characteristics you inherited from your parents at the moment your father's sperm fused with your mother's egg, and the way in which the circumstances and conditions of your upbringing have shaped you.

Some characteristics are decided purely by inheritance, and some purely by your environment. Others are a combination of both ...

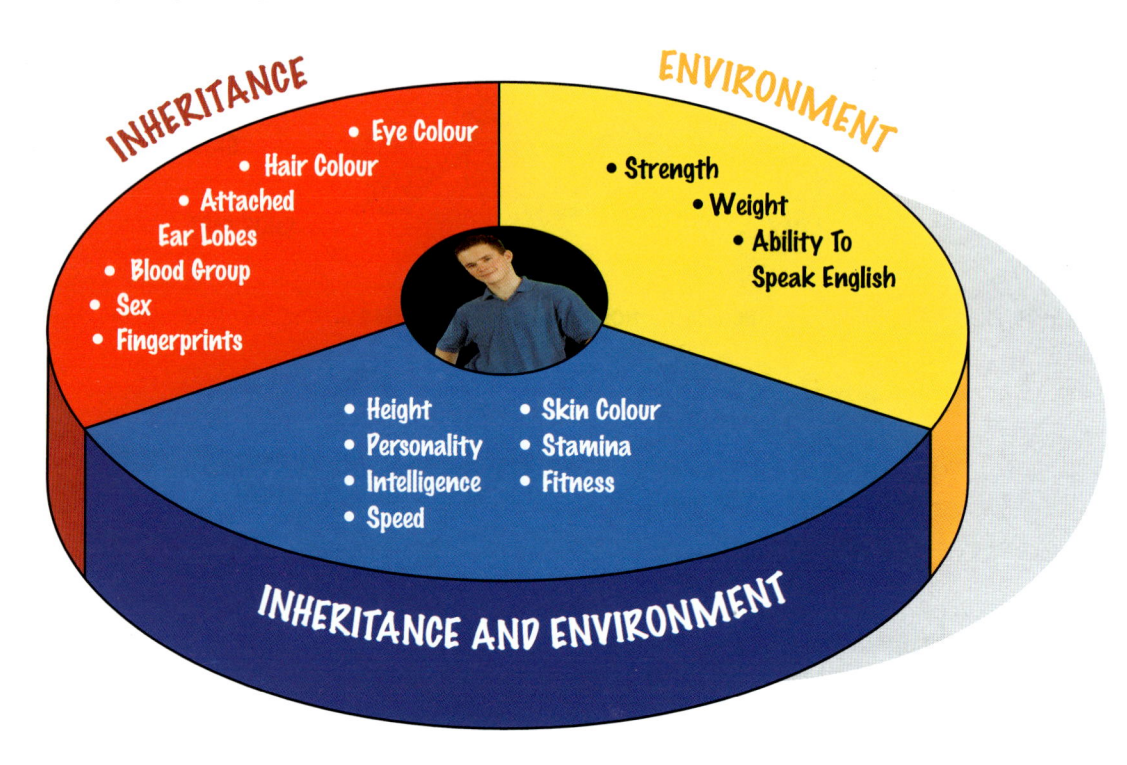

INHERITANCE
- Eye Colour
- Hair Colour
- Attached Ear Lobes
- Blood Group
- Sex
- Fingerprints

ENVIRONMENT
- Strength
- Weight
- Ability To Speak English

INHERITANCE AND ENVIRONMENT
- Height
- Personality
- Intelligence
- Speed
- Skin Colour
- Stamina
- Fitness

HOW ENVIRONMENT CAN AFFECT ORGANISMS

Plants are even more affected by the environment than animals ...

Lack of sunlight ...   Lack of nutrients ...   Lack of water ...

... all reduce the size and health of the plant.

Lack of food  ...   Too much food 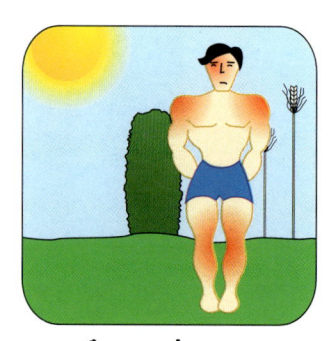 ...   Too much sun ...

GROUPING ANIMALS

Variation and Classification 3

SORTING THINGS OUT

There are so many different types of animals and plants that they need to be sorted out into groups so that we can find what we are looking for?
Those with **WINGS** could go into one group, and those without into another.
Perhaps we could group them by whether they have **0,2,4,6** or **8** legs??
There are many ways but you have to use characteristics that animals have in common. This tends to group animals which are reasonably closely related.

CLASSIFICATION

This means sorting animals out into groups based on their relationship to one another using things that you can see.
So for instance we might put 2 animals into the same big group because they each have 6 legs, 3 sections to their bodies and wings. Get it?
To do this properly we need to know some scientific names for various bits and pieces ...

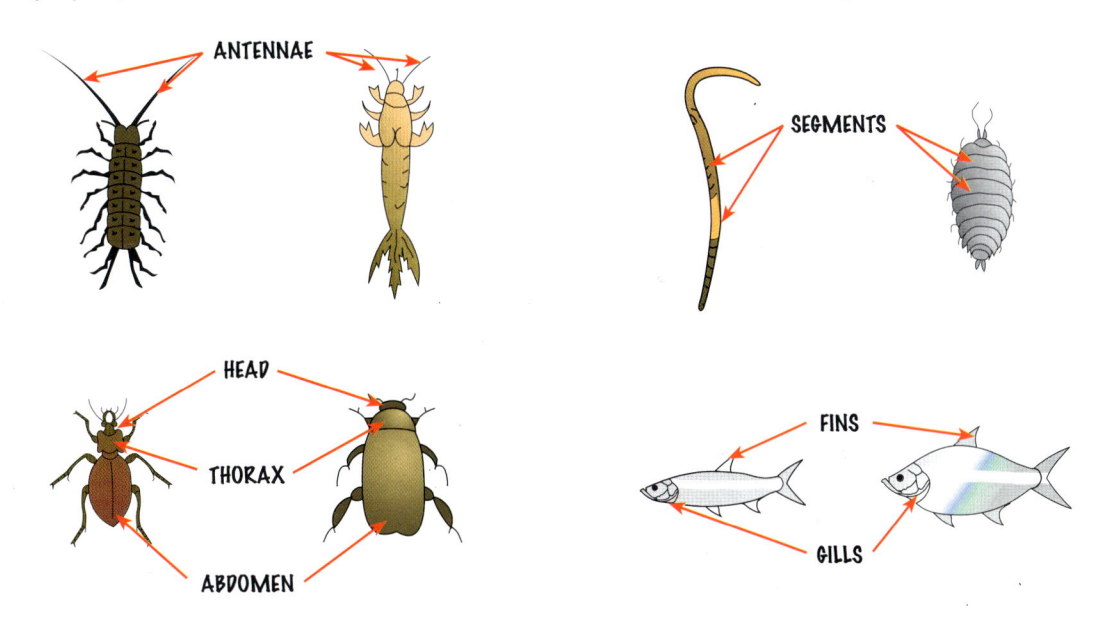

ANTENNAE

SEGMENTS

HEAD
THORAX
ABDOMEN

FINS
GILLS

Now that you know these names have another go at sorting the animals out!

Lonsdale Science Revision Guides

CLASSIFICATION

Variation and Classification — 4

THE MAJOR GROUPS

Basically living things can be divided into two massive groups...
... GREEN PLANTS ...
... and ANIMALS.
These groups can be further broken down into smaller sub-groups. For instance animals can be divided into...
... INVERTEBRATES (without backbones)...
... and VERTEBRATES (with backbones).
These groups can be further sub-divided and so on, and so on...
This system enables scientists to study the relationship between various organisms as well as making identification much easier.

THE INVERTEBRATES - Animals without backbones

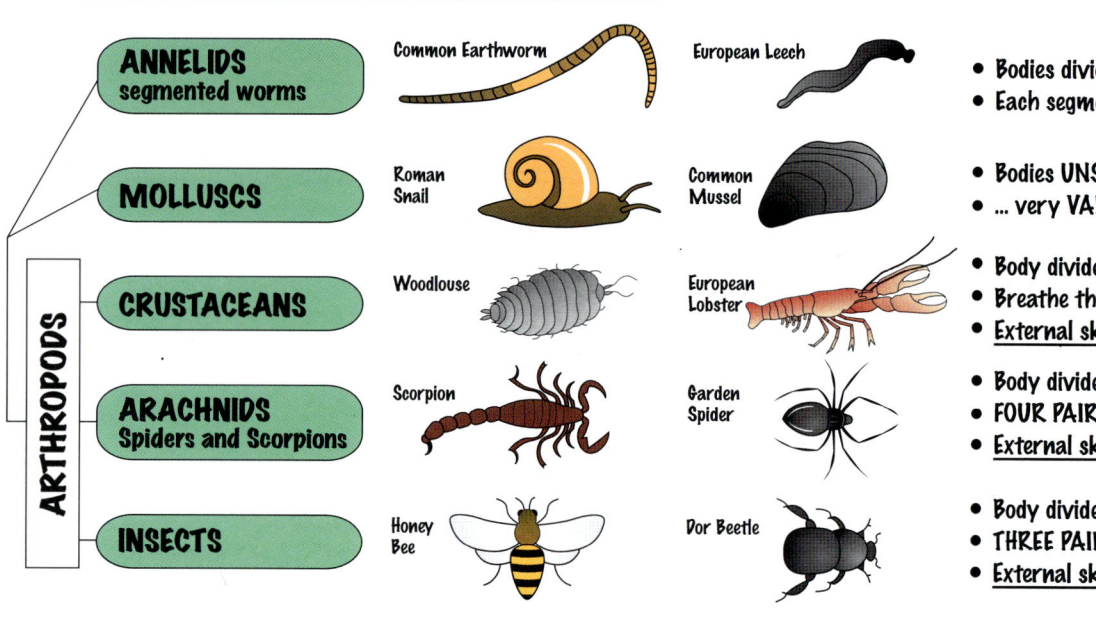

ANNELIDS — segmented worms
Common Earthworm, European Leech
- Bodies divided into SEGMENTS.
- Each segment has BRISTLES.

MOLLUSCS
Roman Snail, Common Mussel
- Bodies UNSEGMENTED and ...
- ... very VARIABLE in shape!!

ARTHROPODS:

CRUSTACEANS
Woodlouse, European Lobster
- Body divided into 3 PARTS.
- Breathe through GILLS.
- External skeleton; jointed legs.

ARACHNIDS — Spiders and Scorpions
Scorpion, Garden Spider
- Body divided into 2 PARTS.
- FOUR PAIRS OF LEGS: no wings.
- External skeleton; jointed legs.

INSECTS
Honey Bee, Dor Beetle
- Body divided into 3 PARTS.
- THREE PAIRS OF LEGS: wings.
- External skeleton; jointed legs.

THE VERTEBRATES - Animals with backbones

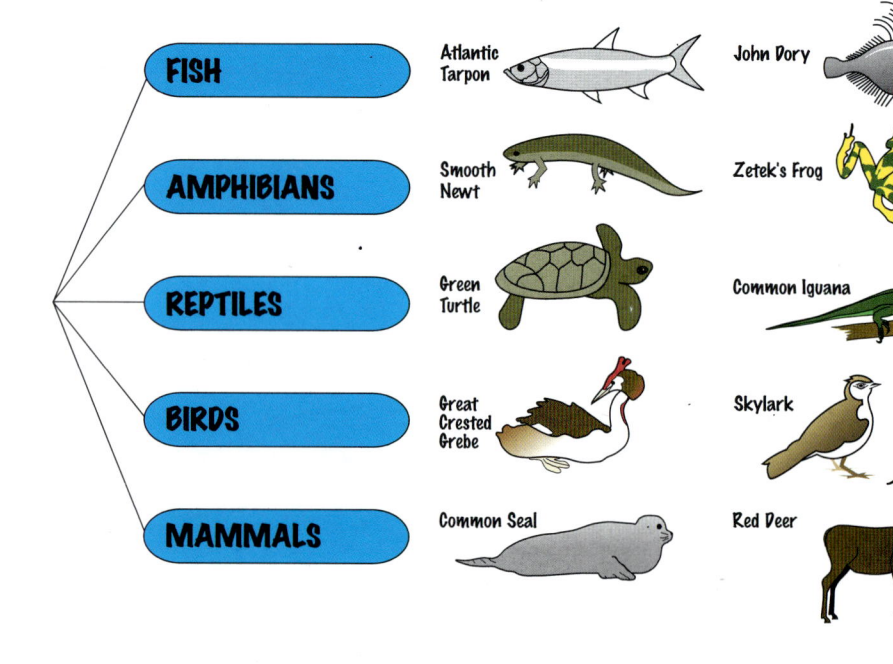

FISH
Atlantic Tarpon, John Dory
- Covered with SCALES.
- Have fins and GILLS.

AMPHIBIANS
Smooth Newt, Zetek's Frog
- Breathe through MOIST SKIN and lungs.
- Need WATER TO BREED.

REPTILES
Green Turtle, Common Iguana
- Have DRY SCALY SKINS.
- Breathe only through LUNGS.

BIRDS
Great Crested Grebe, Skylark
- Have FEATHERS and WINGS.
- Have BEAKS and no teeth.

MAMMALS
Common Seal, Red Deer
- Covered in HAIR (even us!)
- SUCKLE their young.

KEYWORDS AND COMPREHENSION

Variation and Classification — 5

KEYWORDS

Match the keywords from this unit to their definitions ...

#	Keyword	Definition	Answer
1	VARIATION	Animals which don't have a backbone	4 ✓
2	CLASSIFICATION	Worms whose bodies are divided into segments	5 ✓
3	VERTEBRATES	Three parts to the body. Breathe through gills	7 ✓
4	INVERTEBRATES	Two parts to the body. Four pairs of legs	8 ✓
5	ANNELIDS	Breathe through moist skin and lungs. Need water to breed	11 ✓
6	MOLLUSCS	Have feathers, wings and beaks	13 ✓
7	CRUSTACEANS	Have hair and suckle their young	14 ✓
8	ARACHNIDS	Have unsegmented bodies which can be very variable in shape	6 ✓
9	INSECTS	Have dry scaly skin and breathe through lungs	12 ✓
10	FISH	Differences between animals of the same species	1 ✓
11	AMPHIBIANS	Animals which have a backbone	3 ✓
12	REPTILES	Grouping animals using features they have in common	2 ✓
13	BIRDS	Three parts to the body. Three pairs of legs	9 ✓
14	MAMMALS	Covered with scales. Have fins and gills	10 ✓

CLASSIFICATION

Read this passage and then answer the questions below.

A classic case of classification is the way in which products are organised in a supermarket. If you want tinned soup you go to the 'tinned foods' shelves, find the shelf with tinned soups and then go to the brand you want. Simple but effective! Classification of living organisms relies on much the same principles to manage all the billions of different species on our planet. First you might decide that what you're trying to classify is an animal, and also a vertebrate, and maybe you can decide that it is a bird. After that, you may need help to place it more accurately into the category of hawks. Ultimately you should be able to determine its species. e.g. Peregrine falcon. Classification by these methods groups together organisms with similar characteristics. In other words they're closely related to each other in the sense that a Peregrine falcon is more closely related to a Kestrel than an Ostrich (or even a Woodlouse!).

1. Why wouldn't grouping animals by colour be a reasonable method of classification?
2. Why wouldn't grouping animals by name be a reasonable method of classification?
3. If you found a new specimen in a tropical forest, what immediate questions might you want to ask in order to begin classifying it?
4. As the groups get smaller and smaller what would you expect to see in the organisms within the group?
5. What would a scientist have to prove to show that the organism he had discovered was a new species?

TESTING UNDERSTANDING

Variation and Classification — 6

DIFFERENCES BETWEEN INDIVIDUALS

There are very obvious differences between animals and plants of different ....

However there are also .... between organisms of the same ....

These differences are called .... , and this is caused by .... , ... or quite

often a combination of the two. Inherited characteristics include eye colour, hair colour and .... group.

Characteristics influenced by the environment include strength, weight and ability to speak a particular language.

Characteristics which are influenced by both include .... , ... and ....

Organisms of different species can be .... into groups based on their observable ....

Animals with backbones are called .... while those without backbones are ....

These massive groups are further broken down into more closely related groups such as those invertebrates

with jointed legs. These are called .... and are further divided into .... , ...

and .... Similarly the vertebrates are sub-divided into 5 major groups .... ,

.... , ... , ... and ....

CORRELATIONS

A Correlation is just another name for a link between two different things. Here we're investigating the correlation between handspan and armspan

1. How many people are included in this survey?

   ....

2. Do all people with long arms have big hands?

   ....

3. Put a circle around a person with long arms and small hands.

4. Put a circle around a person with short arms and big hands.

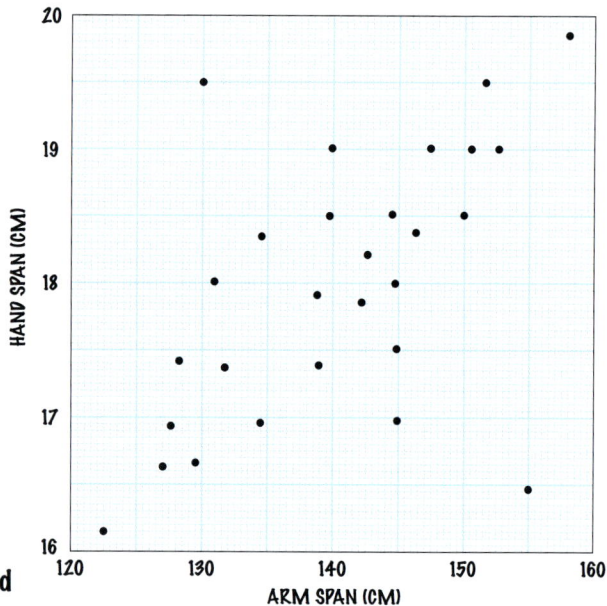

5. Draw a line from the person nearest the bottom left hand corner of the graph to the person nearest the top right hand corner.

6. How many people are above this line? ....

7. How many people are below this line? ....

8. What can you say about the people who are closest to this line?

   ....

9. What can you say about the people who are furthest from this line?

   ....

SCIENTIFIC INVESTIGATION

Variation and Classification — 7

A group of year 7 pupils wanted to perform an investigation into the variation in height amongst year 7 and year 8 pupils. They decided to choose 30 pupils from each group and measure them. There were approximately 180 pupils in each year. Here are their results ...

YEAR 7 (measured in cm)
153, 177, 159, 154, 160, 164, 170, 175, 176, 176, 175, 168, 163, 156, 156, 162, 168, 174, 173, 168, 162, 162, 167, 172, 171, 166, 161, 161, 166, 166.

YEAR 8 (measured in cm)
161, 166, 171, 176, 181, 182, 178, 172, 166, 163, 159, 160, 164, 167, 172, 178, 183, 178, 173, 167, 165, 169, 174, 179, 180, 174, 170, 170, 175, 175.

Tally these figures in rough according to the groupings below and then ...
Plot them on the graph paper below as two separate bar charts ...

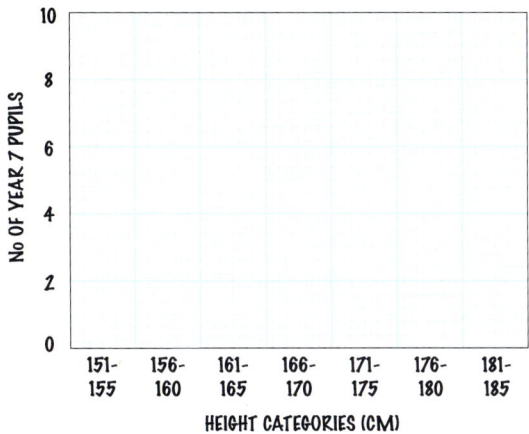

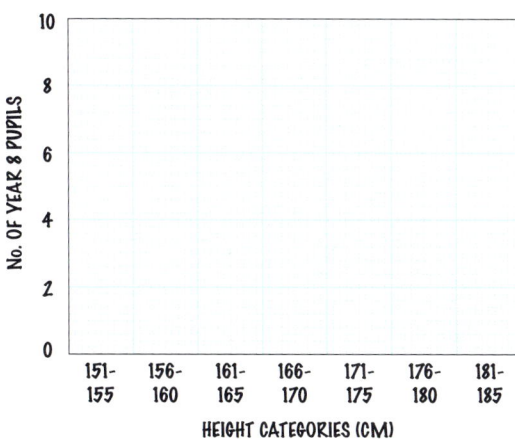

1. What would you have to do to make sure that your comparison was a fair one?

2. What conclusion can you draw from the results of this investigation?

3. If you were to repeat this investigation, how would you improve it?

4. What sort of results would you expect if you compared the variation of height of right-handed people with that of left-handed people?

5. What sort of results would you expect if you compared the heights of pupils who play in the basketball teams with those who don't?

CHARACTERISTICS OF ACIDS AND ALKALIS

Acids and Alkalis 1

CHARACTERISTICS OF ACIDS

ACIDS HAVE A LOW pH – BELOW 7.

ALL ACIDS HAVE A SOUR TASTE. THE WORD COMES FROM A LATIN WORD MEANING SOUR – BUT PLEASE DON'T TEST THIS.

ACIDS CAN BE NEUTRALISED (CANCELLED OUT) BY ALKALIS

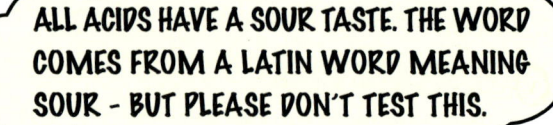

"STRONG" ACIDS ARE CORROSIVE (THEY DISSOLVE THINGS!!)

WEAK ACIDS INCLUDE LEMON JUICE AND VINEGAR

STRONG ACIDS INCLUDE BATTERY ACID, + STOMACH + LABORATORY ACIDS.

CHARACTERISTICS OF ALKALIS

ALKALIS HAVE A HIGH pH – ABOVE 7.

ALKALIS PRODUCE A SOAPY FEEL BETWEEN THE FINGERS (CAREFUL!)

ALKALIS CAN BE NEUTRALISED (CANCELLED OUT) BY ACIDS

'STRONG' ALKALIS CAN BE CORROSIVE (THEY DISSOLVE THINGS!)

WEAK ALKALIS INCLUDE WASHING UP LIQUID AND SOAP

STRONG ALKALIS INCLUDE POWERFUL CLEANING AGENTS AND LABORATORY ALKALIS

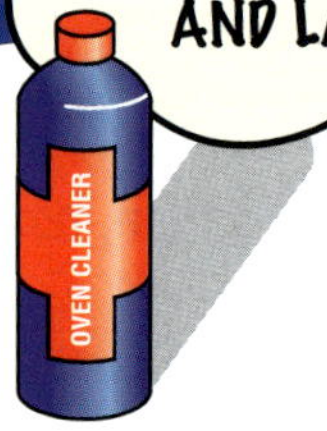

NEUTRAL SUBSTANCES

NEUTRAL SUBSTANCES ARE NEITHER ACIDIC NOR ALKALINE

NEUTRAL SUBSTANCES HAVE A pH OF 7

BECAUSE A SUBSTANCE IS NEUTRAL IT DOESN'T MEAN IT ISN'T HARMFUL!)

NEUTRAL SUBSTANCES INCLUDE PURE WATER

HAZARDOUS SUBSTANCES

Acids and Alkalis — 2

IMPORTANT WARNING

Although many household materials contain acids and alkalis and are not hazardous, you must never taste or touch anything unless told to do so by your teacher!!!

ALWAYS WEAR GOGGLES!

DON'T TASTE    DON'T TOUCH

Several of the substances that we use in the laboratory are kept in containers which have special warning symbols. These are called HAZARD SYMBOLS and three of the most important in this list are shown in the diagram opposite ...
HARMFUL, CORROSIVE and IRRITANT.

Harmful substances are similar to toxic substances but less dangerous.

Corrosive substances attack and destroy living tissues, including eyes and skin.

Irritants are not corrosive but can cause reddening or blistering of the skin.

WHAT TO DO WITH SPILLS

First of all if there's even a bottle of acid on the bench you must be wearing goggles. Eyes are very precious and very delicate. If however, an accident happens and acid or alkali is spilled, do the following:

1. DON'T PANIC - BUT DO TELL YOUR TEACHER IMMEDIATELY.
2. GET LOTS OF WATER FROM THE TAP AND POUR IT GENTLY ONTO THE SPILLAGE.
3. IF ACID OR ALKALI IS ON SOMEONE'S SKIN, RUN LOTS OF COLD WATER OVER IT.

Adding water dilutes acids and alkalis and makes them less HARMFUL, less CORROSIVE and less IRRITANT.

HAZCARDS AND HAZARD WARNING SIGNS

Hazcards will tell you the risks associated with any chemical you use. Your teacher will show you some ...

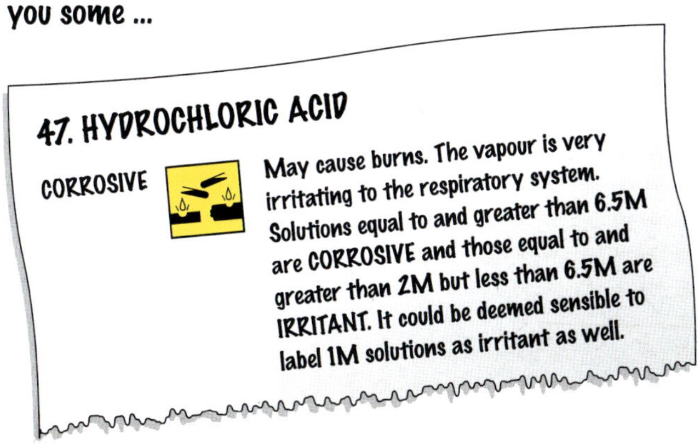

47. HYDROCHLORIC ACID

CORROSIVE

May cause burns. The vapour is very irritating to the respiratory system. Solutions equal to and greater than 6.5M are CORROSIVE and those equal to and greater than 2M but less than 6.5M are IRRITANT. It could be deemed sensible to label 1M solutions as irritant as well.

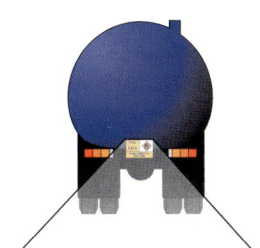

When dangerous chemicals are transported the vehicles must carry hazard information panels in case of an accident ...

3YE
1270
CLEMAN CHEMICAL Co.
01257 372410

Lonsdale Science Revision Guides

INDICATORS

Acids and Alkalis — 3

NATURAL INDICATORS

Because some acids and alkalis are either HARMFUL, IRRITANT or CORROSIVE, we can't go around tasting or feeling substances to find out which they are!

Happily, there are some substances which actually change colour in acids or alkalis.

We call them INDICATORS and they are often natural materials such as red cabbage, raw beetroot, blackcurrant, bilberries, blackberries and onion skins.

LITMUS is a very common indicator made from Lichens!

- When an acid is added to blue Litmus it turns red.
- When an alkali is added to red Litmus it turns blue.
- When either are added to a neutral substance there is no colour change.

Litmus is often absorbed onto paper called 'Litmus Paper' to make it more convenient to use.

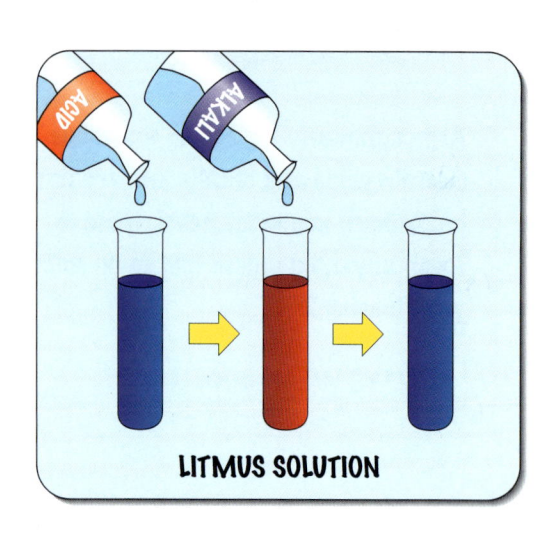

LITMUS SOLUTION

UNIVERSAL INDICATOR AND pH

UNIVERSAL INDICATOR is a mixture of dyes which can produce a range of different colours depending on the STRENGTH of the acid or alkali being tested. It can also be absorbed onto paper to make testing a bit easier. We measure the strength of an acid or alkali using the pH SCALE.

This is a continuous scale from 1-14. pH 7 is neutral.

VERY ACIDIC					SLIGHTLY ACIDIC	NEUTRAL	SLIGHTLY ALKALINE					VERY ALKALINE
1	2	3	4	5	6	7	8	9	10	11	12	13	14

When used with UNIVERSAL INDICATOR, we get the following range of colours:-

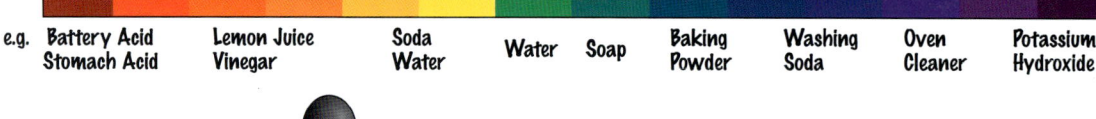

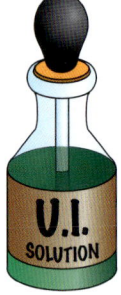

e.g. Battery Acid / Stomach Acid — Lemon Juice / Vinegar — Soda Water — Water — Soap — Baking Powder — Washing Soda — Oven Cleaner — Potassium Hydroxide

pH AND CORROSIVENESS

Acids become more and more CORROSIVE as their pH falls. Acids with a pH of 1 or 2 are much more corrosive than those with a pH of 5 or 6.

Similarly, Alkalis become more corrosive as their pH rises. Alkalis with a pH of 13 or 14 are much more corrosive than those with a pH of 8 or 9.

NEUTRALISATION AND USES

Acids and Alkalis — 4

NEUTRALISATION

Because acids and alkalis are 'CHEMICAL OPPOSITES' they can be used to cancel each other out, or NEUTRALISE each other.

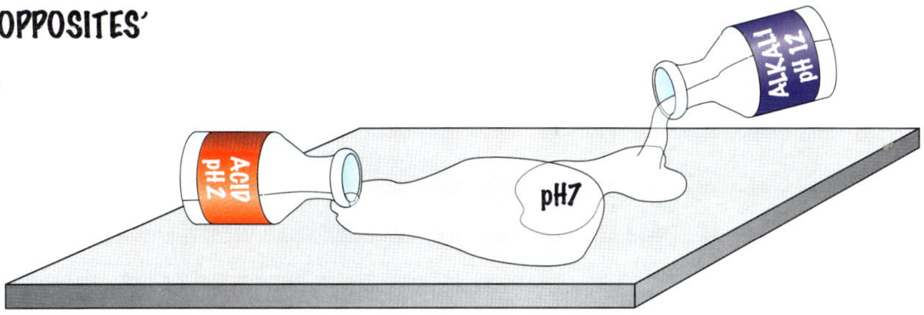

As alkali is added to the split acid ...
... the pH starts to increase.

If the correct amount of alkali is added, the pH will reach 7, neutrality. If more is added, then the solution will become more and more alkaline.

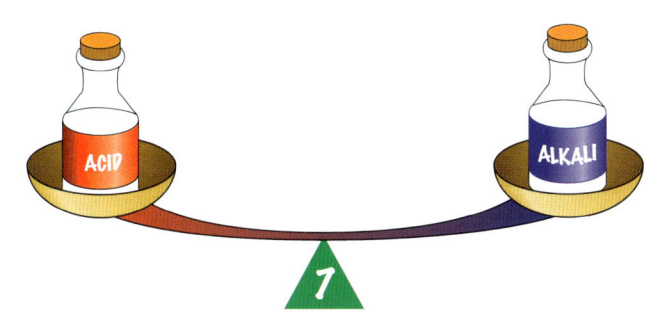

NEUTRALISATION will happen only if the right amounts of acid and alkali are used.

EVERYDAY USES OF ACIDS AND ALKALIS

FOOD PRESERVATION
- Food can be made to last longer by 'pickling'. This means storing in vinegar (ethanoic acid).
- The acid stops bacteria from multiplying and decaying the food.

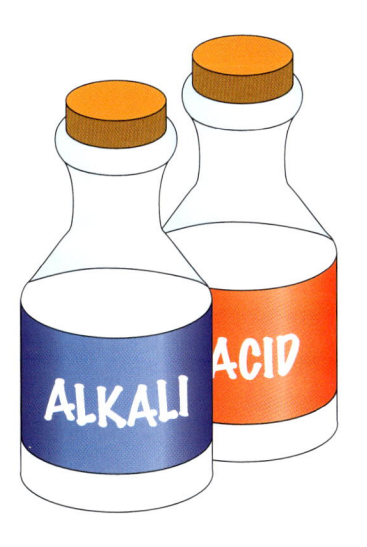

DIGESTION AND INDIGESTION
- The human stomach produces quite a strong acid to help in digestion. If it produces too much we get 'acid indigestion' or heartburn, and have to take a mild alkali in the form of an ANTACID.

SOIL TREATMENT
- Different plants prefer different soil pH's. Some are acid-loving and some are alkali-loving.
- Soil pH can be changed by adding lime or mildly acidic compounds.

STING BITES
- Bee stings are acidic and should be neutralised be applying a mild antacid (washing soda).
- Wasp stings are alkaline and need to be treated with vinegar.

HAIR AND SKIN CARE
- Shampoos tend to be alkaline so that they can remove grease. After shampooing, a conditioner will neutralise the pH of the hair.
- After using a cleanser on your face its a good idea to use a 'pH balanced' Moisturiser.

KEYWORDS AND COMPREHENSION

Acids and Alkalis — 5

KEYWORDS

Match the keywords from this unit to their definitions ...

ACIDIC	The 'cancelling out' of an acid by an alkali, or vice versa
ALKALINE	A substance which has a pH of 7
pH SCALE	A substance which can cause blistering of the skin
NEUTRALISATION	Contains information on the risks associated with certain chemicals
NEUTRAL	These give an immediate warning of hazardous substances
CORROSIVE	A mixture of indicators which gives a range of colour over different pH's
IRRITANT	A substance which can be used to neutralize an acid e.g. in indigestion
HARMFUL	A substance with a pH less than 7
HAZCARD	Substances which change colour in the presence of acid and alkali
HAZARD SYMBOLS	A scale from 1-14 which measures acidity and alkalinity
INDICATORS	An indicator which is red in acid and blue in alkali
UNIVERSAL INDICATOR	A substance which attacks living materials (and some metals and rocks)
LITMUS	A substance which is dangerous to touch or inhale
ANTACID	A substance with a pH more than 7

DANGEROUS CARGOS

Read this passage and then answer the questions below.

Dangerous chemicals such as strong acids and alkalis should really be transported by rail but unfortunately they are more often transported by special tankers on public highways. Because of this, special warnings and information have to be visible on the tanker in case of accident. Part of this information deals with the way the fire brigade are allowed to deal with a severe spillage. There are 4 alternatives: (a) Waterjets, (b) waterfog (c) foam and (d) dry agent which are indicated by a simple code number. Another vital piece of information concerns the name of the hazardous substance. Again this is indicated by a unique number (e.g. 1270 is petrol) alongside the name of the chemical manufacturer. Further instructions, to DILUTE or CONTAIN the spillage, to wear breathing apparatus or to use full body protective clothing also appear on the hazard warning. The letter 'E' stands for 'CONSIDER EVACUATION' of people nearby!

1. Where should the warning sign (s) be placed on the tanker for easy viewing?
2. What disadvantage would there be in using water jets?
3. If there was a steady leakage of acid what would you send for if you were first on the scene?
4. What advantage would there be in diluting an acid spill?
5. Do you think it's acceptable to allow dangerous chemicals to be transported on public highways?

TESTING UNDERSTANDING

Acids and Alkalis — 6

DANGEROUS LIQUIDS

Acids have a .... taste, have a .... less than .... , and if 'strong' enough are .... Alkalis feel .... between the fingers (careful!), have a .... greater than .... and are also .... if in a 'strong' enough concentration. .... substances have a pH of seven.

Both acids and alkalis can be harmful and also an .... to the skin. If you spill either of them onto yourself you <u>must</u> run the affected area under as much cold .... as possible to .... the acid or alkali.

.... can be used to distinguish between acids and alkalis. Litmus simply turns .... in acid and .... in alkali, but Universal Indicator is a .... of dyes which produce a range of .... depending on the .... of the substance being tested.

If an acid is added to an alkali, the two substances will .... each other, and may result in a substance with a pH of .... This process is used to reduce excess acid in the stomach by taking ....

ADDING ACID TO ALKALIS

Some students used a piece of apparatus called a burette to add acid to alkali in a beaker. They added Universal Indicator Solution to the alkali at the start of the experiment and then estimated the pH by gauging the colour of the liquid. They constantly stirred the liquid.

Vol. OF ACID ADDED (cm³)	0	8	24	60	100
pH OF SOLUTION	14	12	10	8	7

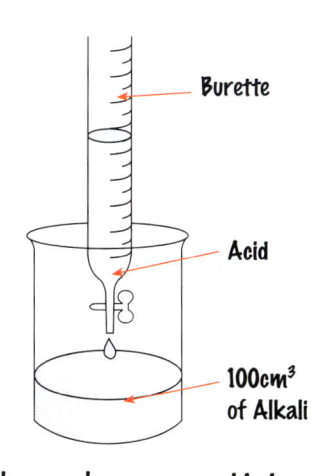

Plot these results onto the graph paper provided

1. What colour was the solution at the start?

2. What was the final colour of the solution?

3. Which was the 'stronger,' the acid or the alkali? Explain your answer.

SCIENTIFIC INVESTIGATION
Acids and Alkalis — 7

A group of students decided to investigate the effectiveness of a group of different antacid powders. These were used to treat indigestion and the pupils were trying to find out how much acid each sample would neutralise. They did this by adding 4g of each antacid, 1g at a time, to 25cm³ of acid of pH2. They monitored the pH using a pH meter and recorded these results.
Put them into the table opposite

A pH2, pH3, pH4, pH5, pH6
B pH2, pH4, pH6, pH7, pH7
C pH2, pH2, pH3, pH3, pH4
D pH2, pH5, pH7, pH7, pH7
E pH2, pH2, pH2, pH3, pH3

SUBSTANCE	pH after 0g				

Plot these as 5 different lines on the graph opposite

1. What factors would have to be kept the same in this investigation in order to make it a fair test?

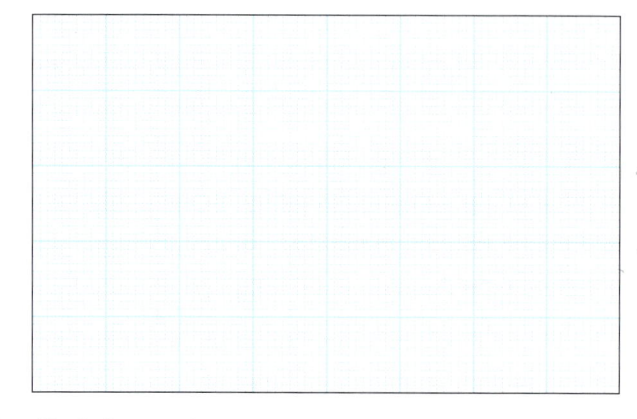

2. Which of these substances has the greatest effect on the pH of the acid?

3. Which of these substances reduces the pH of the acid the fastest?

4. Which of these substances has the least effect on the pH of the acid?

5. What pH would you get if you added 1.5g of the substance D to the acid?

6. What pH would you get if you added 2.5g of substance E to the acid?

7. What amount of substance A would need to be added to get a pH of 5.5?

8. "Quick" antacids produce a lot of gas quickly. Which therefore would you choose as an ideal antacid?

REACTIONS OF ACIDS WITH METALS

Simple Chemical Reactions — 1

A WORD ABOUT CHEMICAL REACTIONS

In chemical reactions chemical changes occur which are IRREVERSIBLE.
In other words they are difficult to reverse or undo!

When a chemical reaction happens there are often some 'tell tale' signs ...
- There may be bubbling or fizzing ...
- There may be heat given off ...
- There may be a colour change ...
- A solution may go cloudy.

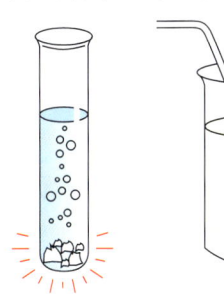

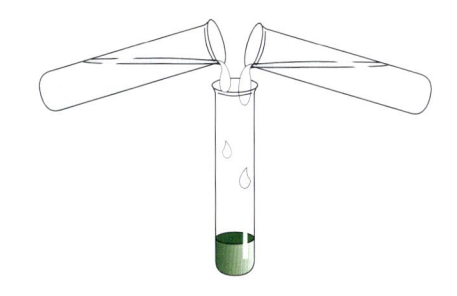

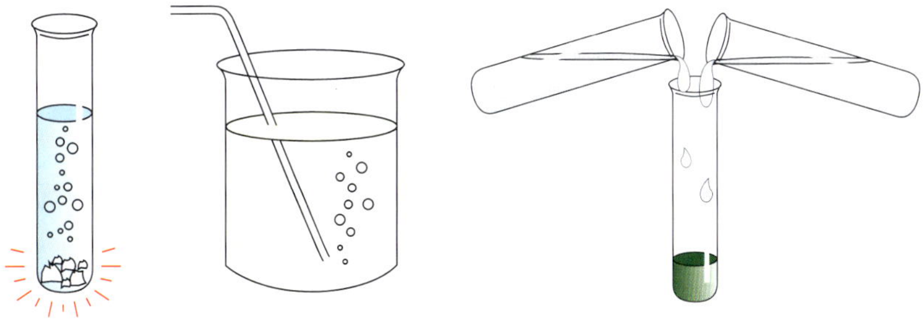

In all chemical reactions you start off with a substance or substances (the REACTANTS)
and end up with a new substance or substances (the PRODUCTS).

ADDING ACIDS TO METALS

PLEASE WEAR GOGGLES

If a normal laboratory acid such as dilute hydrochloric acid is added to magnesium, zinc, iron or tin a reaction will occur and HYDROGEN gas will be produced.
It can be collected as shown in the diagram below.

- When the acid is added to the metal in the flask bubbles start to appear ...
- ... and the metal starts to disappear if there is enough acid.
- The metal is being CORRODED away.

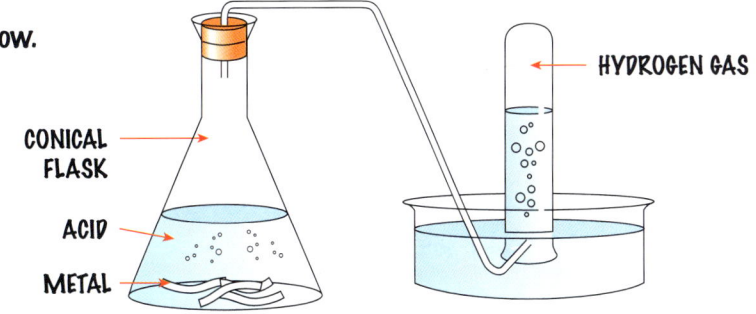

CONICAL FLASK
ACID
METAL
HYDROGEN GAS

In other words a chemical reaction is occurring and one of the products is hydrogen

However ...
Some metals such as copper, silver and gold are so UNREACTIVE that they just will not react with acid.
If you try adding acid to them you will not get a single bubble of hydrogen.

TESTING FOR HYDROGEN GAS

The test for hydrogen can be a bit alarming if you haven't done it before!

- Take a test tube of hydrogen gas ...
- ... keeping the mouth of the tube downwards ...
- ... and place a lighted taper at the mouth of the tube.
- Hydrogen produces a high pitched 'squeaky pop' as the gas ignites (catches fire)

Test for hydrogen gas

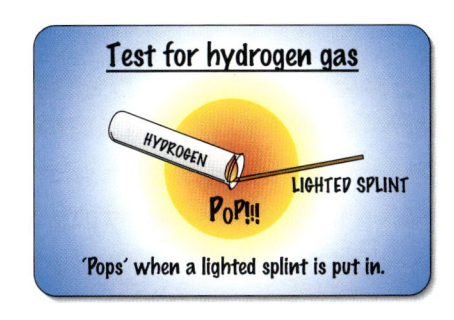

HYDROGEN
LIGHTED SPLINT
PoP!!!

'Pops' when a lighted splint is put in.

Lonsdale Science Revision Guides

39

REACTIONS OF ACIDS WITH CARBONATES

Simple Chemical Reactions — 2

EXAMPLES OF CARBONATES

- CARBONATES are chemical compounds which contain carbon and oxygen.
- You will be familiar with several common carbonates ...
  ... such as limestone rocks, chalk, marble, baking powder and some indigestion remedies.
- Carbonates have one very important thing in common ...
  ... they all fizz like mad and give off bubbles if you add acid to them.

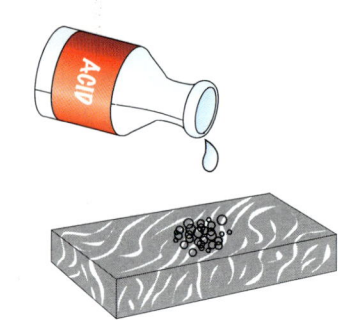

ADDING ACIDS TO CARBONATES

PLEASE WEAR GOGGLES

When a normal laboratory acid such as dilute hydrochloric acid is added to any carbonate, a reaction will occur and CARBON DIOXIDE gas will be produced.
It can be collected as shown in the diagram below,
because it is heavier than air and can be collected directly into a test tube.

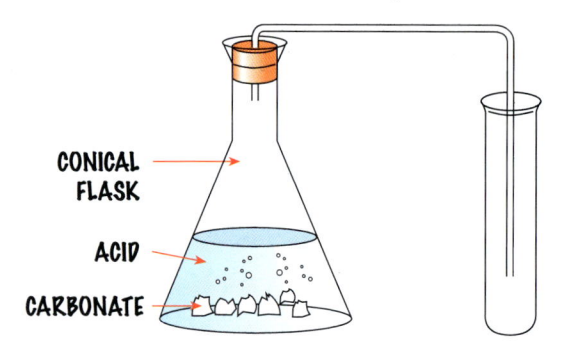

- CONICAL FLASK
- ACID
- CARBONATE

- When the acid is added to the carbonate in the flask bubbles start to appear ...
- ... and the carbonate starts to get 'worn away' if there is enough acid.
- Acid rain does this to some buildings.

In other words a chemical reaction has taken place and one of the products is carbon dioxide.

TESTING FOR CARBON DIOXIDE GAS

To test for carbon dioxide, you need to use a harmless substance called LIMEWATER.
- If carbon dioxide is bubbled directly into limewater ...
- ... it goes MILKY.

This is a positive test for carbon dioxide
- and yet another example of a chemical reaction.

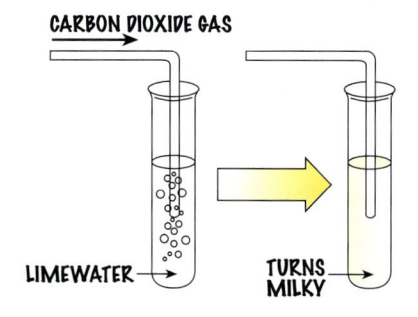

CARBON DIOXIDE GAS
LIMEWATER → TURNS MILKY

COMPARING CARBON DIOXIDE TO HYDROGEN

Although these are both colourless gases with no smell, they have very different properties ...
- Carbon dioxide is heavier than 'air' and puts out fires.
- Hydrogen is lighter than 'air' and burns explosively!!

BURNING

Simple Chemical Reactions — 3

THE PRODUCTS OF BURNING

Oxygen makes up about ⅕th of the air, and it is this substance which supports burning.
Without oxygen, things just won't burn!!
Burning is another type of chemical reaction and is also called **COMBUSTION**.

When a substance burns in air or in oxygen, an **OXIDE** is formed.
In the example shown opposite, the oxide formed is MAGNESIUM OXIDE.

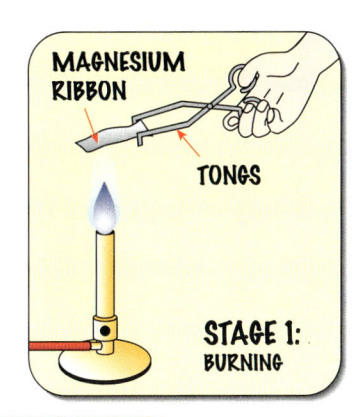

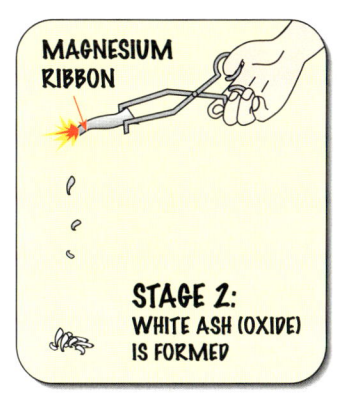

STAGE 1: BURNING — MAGNESIUM RIBBON, TONGS

STAGE 2: WHITE ASH (OXIDE) IS FORMED — MAGNESIUM RIBBON

BURNING IN AIR COMPARED TO BURNING IN OXYGEN

Pure oxygen naturally supports burning better than air since there is five times more oxygen available.
This means that things burn very violently in pure oxygen, and great care must be taken such as wearing goggles, gloves, using tongs and not staring directly at the flame.

Magnesium in a gas jar full of air ... burns brightly.

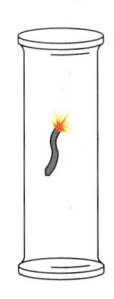

BURNING THINGS IN PURE OXYGEN SHOULD ONLY BE DONE BY YOUR TEACHER!!

Magnesium in a gas jar full of pure oxygen ... burns extremely violently.

WORD EQUATIONS FOR COMBUSTION

MAGNESIUM + OXYGEN → MAGNESIUM <u>OXIDE</u>

SULPHUR + OXYGEN → SULPHUR <u>DIOXIDE</u>

CARBON + OXYGEN → CARBON <u>DIOXIDE</u> (which you can test for using limewater)

FIRE SAFETY

The fire triangle pictured opposite shows the three things which a fire must have.
If one of these is removed then the fire will go out.
This forms the basic principle of fire fighting.

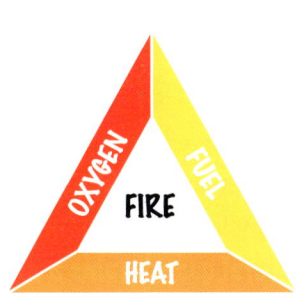

a) **Removing heat:** This is often done by pumping large amounts of water onto the fire e.g. in burning houses etc.

b) **Removing oxygen:** This can be done by smothering the fire in a blanket or using a foam fire extinguisher. In the case of a chip pan fire a damp towel should be placed over the pan.

c) **Removing fuel:** This is more difficult and is usually only tackled by experienced, specialist firefighters.

Fire triangle: OXYGEN / FUEL / HEAT — FIRE

Lonsdale Science Revision Guides

FUELS

Simple Chemical Reactions — 4

EXAMPLES OF FUELS

Fuels are substances which release useful amounts of energy when they burn.
Most of the fuels we use in the world are FOSSIL FUELS, which are formed over millions of years from dead plant and material.

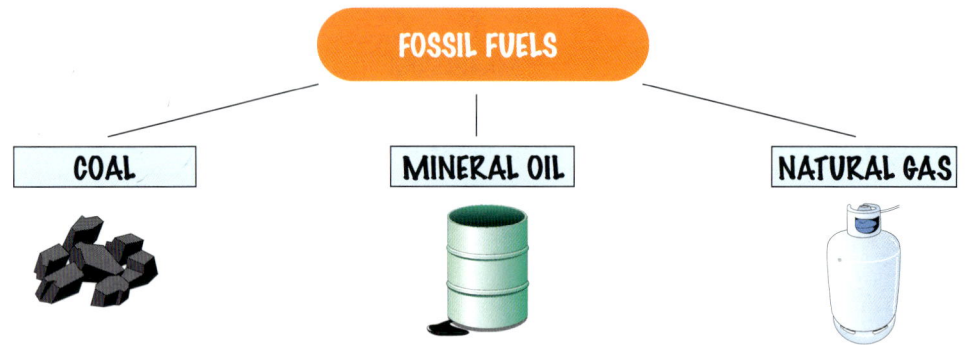

FOSSIL FUELS
- COAL
- MINERAL OIL
- NATURAL GAS

BURNING FOSSIL FUELS

1) **COAL:** Because coal is rich in carbon, burning it produces carbon dioxide.

   CARBON + OXYGEN → CARBON DIOXIDE

2) **OIL AND GAS:** Because both oil and gas are rich in carbon and hydrogen, burning them produces carbon dioxide and water.

   OIL/GAS + OXYGEN → CARBON DIOXIDE + WATER

This also happens when any substances obtained from oil are burned e.g. kerosene, diesel oil, candle wax, petrol etc.
Substances like this containing carbon and hydrogen are called HYDROCARBONS.

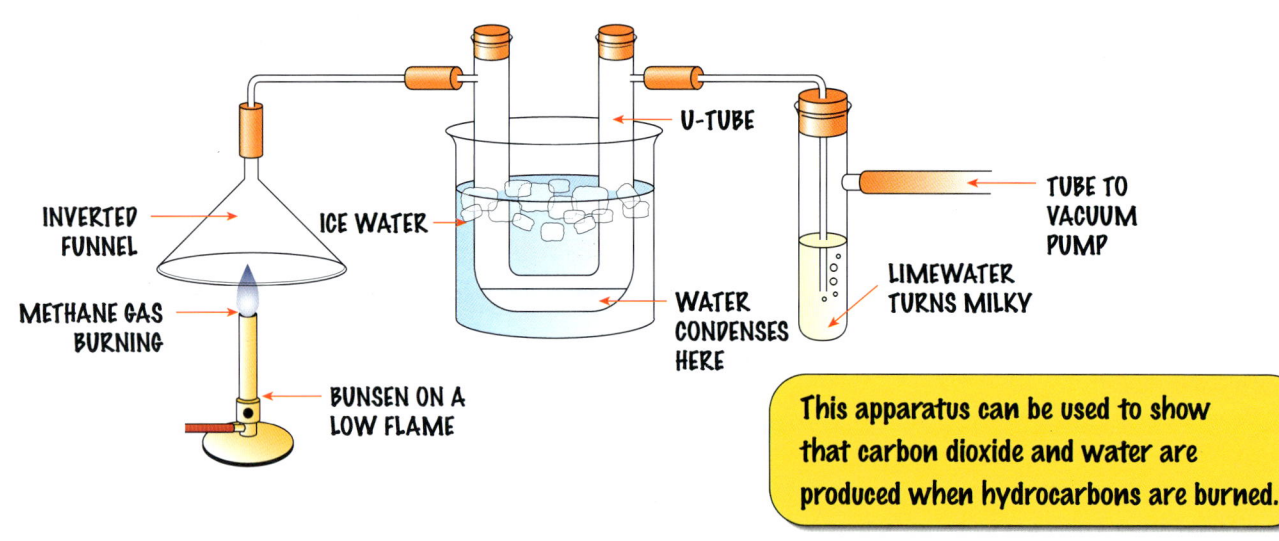

Labels on apparatus diagram: INVERTED FUNNEL, ICE WATER, U-TUBE, TUBE TO VACUUM PUMP, LIMEWATER TURNS MILKY, WATER CONDENSES HERE, METHANE GAS BURNING, BUNSEN ON A LOW FLAME.

This apparatus can be used to show that carbon dioxide and water are produced when hydrocarbons are burned.

- Other hydrocarbons could be used in this demonstration, such as ... candle wax, paraffin and methylated spirits. NEVER USE PETROL
- Natural gas contains a hydrocarbon called METHANE.
- The word equation for burning methane in air is ...

   METHANE + OXYGEN → CARBON DIOXIDE + WATER (VAPOUR)

The water vapour is condensed to water by the ice water, and the carbon dioxide turns limewater milky.

Lonsdale Science Revision Guides

KEYWORDS AND COMPREHENSION

Simple Chemical Reactions — 5

KEYWORDS

Match the keywords from this unit to their definitions ...

IRREVERSIBLE	The substances produced during a chemical reaction
REVERSIBLE	Doesn't react easily with other substances
PRODUCTS	Is turned 'cloudy' when carbon dioxide is bubbled through it
REACTANTS	A chemical reaction better known as burning
CORRODED	A reaction which is easily reversed or undone
UNREACTIVE	Energy rich substance formed over millions of years from dead organisms
CARBONATES	Substances which contain only hydrogen and carbon
LIMEWATER	The hydrocarbon which is found in natural gas
COMBUSTION	Formed when a substance burns in air or in oxygen
OXIDE	Compounds which contain carbon and oxygen which 'fizz' when added to acid
FOSSIL FUEL	'Eaten away' or dissolved, usually by an acid
HYDROCARBONS	A reaction which is very difficult to reverse or undo
METHANE	The substances which react together in a chemical reaction

PHLOGISTON THEORY

Read this passage and then answer the questions below.

Oxygen was discovered by two men independently of each other. Joseph Priestly in England and Carl Scheele in Sweden made the discovery in 1774. During the 18th Century the Phlogiston theory evolved to explain what happened during combustion. Scientists of the time believed that flammable substances contained something call phlogiston which was given off to the atmosphere when a substance was burned. For example when burned, wood became ash plus phlogiston which went off into the air! They used the theory to explain why substances were lighter after they had been burned, and why some substances burned more easily than others. Eventually, scientists led by a Frenchman Antoine Lavoisier showed that substances actually increase in weight when they burn and therefore phlogiston would have to have a negative weight! (i.e. weigh less than nothing!!)

1. Who discovered oxygen and in which year.?
2. What theory was used to explain combustion during the 18th century?
3. How did scientists explain weight loss during burning during the 18th century?
4. Why do you think that early scientists thought that weight was lost when something is burned?
5. How did 18th century scientists explain the fact that somethings burned more easily than others?
6. Why do substances actually increase in weight when they burn?
7. Why did Lavoisier suggest that phlogiston would have to have a negative weight for the theory to be true.

TESTING UNDERSTANDING

Simple Chemical Reactions — 6

REACTING SUBSTANCES

When a .... reaction occurs, new substances are formed. These changes are usually quite hard to .... These types of reaction can sometimes be identified due to .... being given off, or possibly a .... change. Also, a solution may go .... due to a precipitate being formed, or may .... as a gas is given off. After the reaction has happened, the .... formed are often very different from the .... you started with.

A typical .... reaction occurs when a reactive metal is added to dilute .... acid. This results in .... being given off which can be seen as .... coming from the metal. This .... can be collected in a test-tube over water and will give a characteristic .... when a lighted taper is inserted. The amount of .... released in this sort of reaction depends on the amount of .... and .... used in the reaction.

USING MORE REACTANTS

Some pupils used this apparatus to investigate how increasing the amount of metal affected the amount of gas given off. They kept adding acid until the metal had completely disappeared.

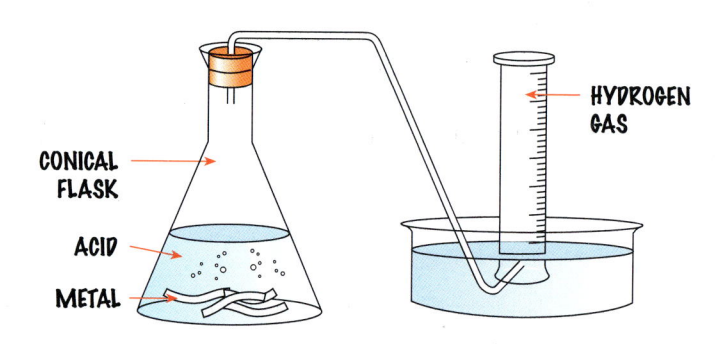

They measured the volume of gas using a graduated gas jar. Here are their results.

MASS OF METAL (g)	0.5	1.0	1.5	2.0	2.5	3.0	3.5	4.0	4.5	5.0
VOL. OF HYDROGEN (cm³)	600	1100	1400	2100	2500	3000	3400	4000	4400	5000

Plot these onto the graph paper alongside. What conclusions can you draw from these results?

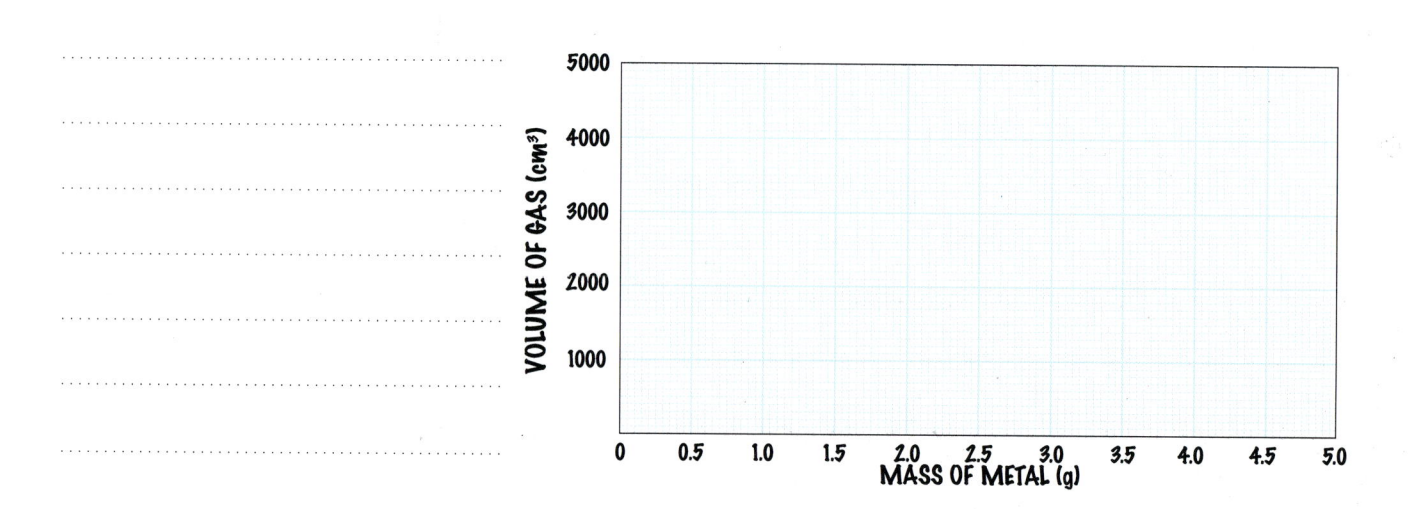

44

SCIENTIFIC INVESTIGATION

Simple Chemical Reactions — 7

Several Year 7 pupils decided to investigate whether there was a link between the amount of time a candle burned in an enclosed space, and the amount of air that was available to it. The equipment they used is shown in the diagram. The bell jar stopper was removed as the bell jar was lowered over the candle, and then immediately replaced as the clock was started. The side of the bell jar was graduated in litres. The pupils got the following results.

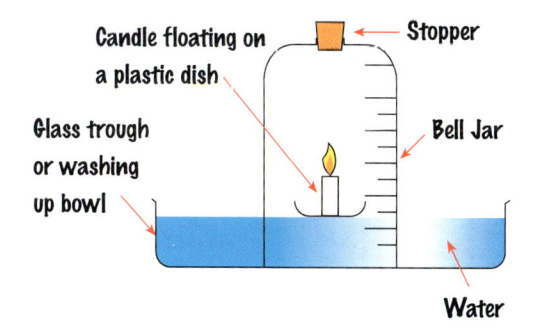

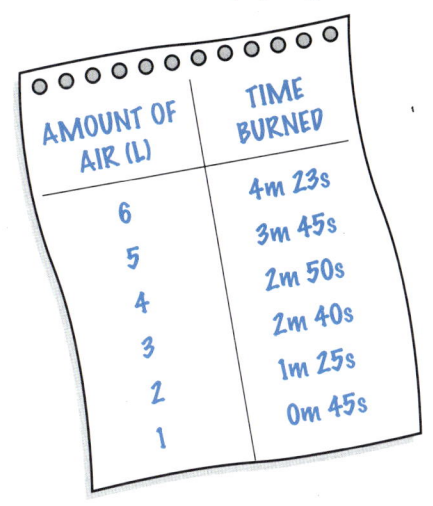

Diagram labels: Candle floating on a plastic dish; Stopper; Glass trough or washing up bowl; Bell Jar; Water

AMOUNT OF AIR (L)	TIME BURNED
6	4m 23s
5	3m 45s
4	2m 50s
3	2m 40s
2	1m 25s
1	0m 45s

Plot these results on the graph provided

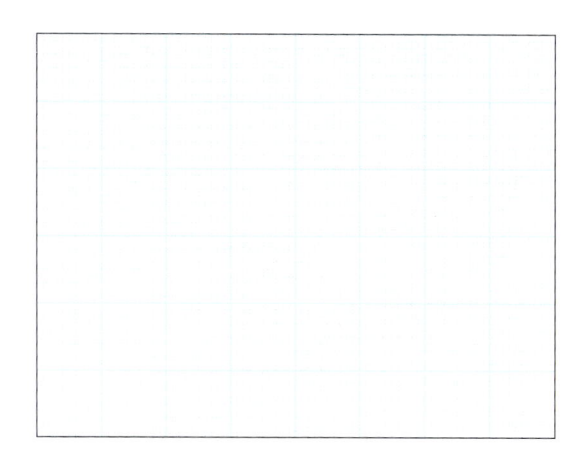

1. Which variables should you control in order to make this a fair test?

2. Which variable is difficult to control using this apparatus and may affect your results?

3. Why did the candle eventually go out?

4. What would happen to the level of water inside the bell jar?

5. Explain your answer to question 4.

6. What conclusions can you draw from this investigation?

7. What substances are produced when a wax candle burns?

8. Do any of the pupils results look wrong? If so, which?

9. Use the graph to work out how long a candle would burn in 2.5 litres of air.

Lonsdale Science Revision Guides — 45

SOLIDS, LIQUIDS AND GASES

Particle Model Of Solids, Liquids And Gases — 1

Everything around us is made up of MATTER which exists as either SOLID, LIQUID or GAS. These are called the THREE STATES OF MATTER, and they have different characteristics.

CAN THEY BE COMPRESSED (SQUASHED)?

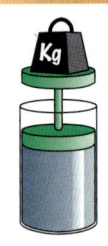

Solids cannot be compressed

Liquids cannot be compressed

Gases can be compressed easily

DO THEY FLOW?

Solids do not flow

Liquids do flow

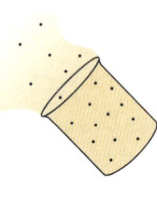

Gases do flow

DO THEY KEEP THEIR SHAPE?

The shape of a solid stays the same

A liquid takes the shape of the bottom of the container

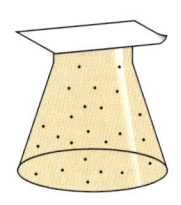

A gas takes the shape of the entire container

DO THEY KEEP THEIR VOLUME?

The volume of a solid stays the same

The volume of a liquid stays the same

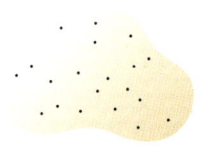

A gas has no definite volume

USING KEYS TO CLASSIFY MATERIALS

One way of classifying a material as either solid, liquid or gas is to use a KEY. If we take the first two properties above then a simple key can be drawn which would enable us to determine the state of any material.
A different key, which would work just as well, can be drawn and used if we take any other two properties.

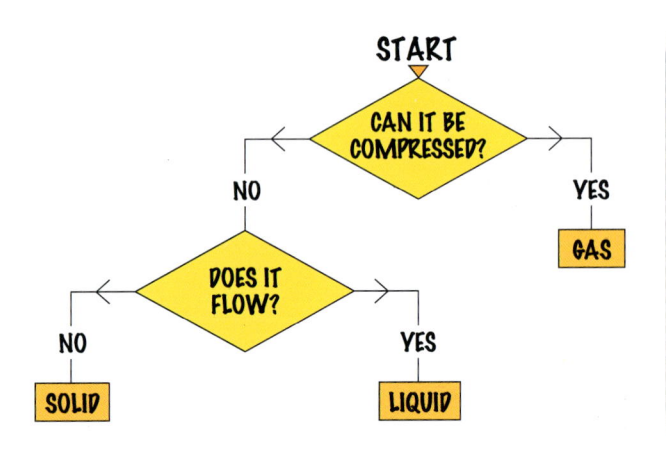

START → CAN IT BE COMPRESSED? → YES: GAS
NO → DOES IT FLOW? → NO: SOLID / YES: LIQUID

MAKING YOUR OWN KEY
- Pick a property that splits the three states into two groups (all the properties above do this).
- This will allow you to identify one particular state.
- You now pick another property which splits the two remaining states.
- Your key is now complete enabling you to classify any material.

46 — Lonsdale Science Revision Guides

PARTICLE THEORY

Particle Model Of Solids, Liquids And Gases — 2

All SOLIDS, LIQUIDS and GASES are made up of VERY SMALL PARTICLES. These particles are far too small for the eye to see. How these particles are ARRANGED and MOVE in each state is known as PARTICLE THEORY.

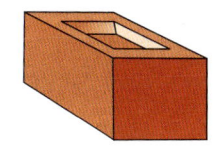

SOLIDS

PARTICLES IN A SOLID LOOK LIKE ...

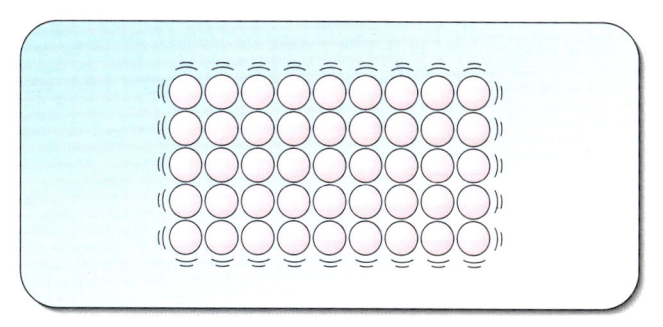

- The particles are VERY CLOSE TOGETHER and each particle exerts a LARGE PULL FORCE on every other particle.
- The particles can ONLY VIBRATE (move to and fro) about their FIXED POSITION which doesn't change.

LIQUIDS

PARTICLES IN A LIQUID LOOK LIKE ...

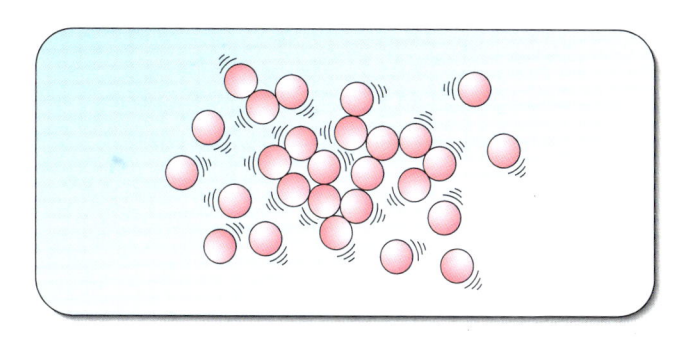

- The particles are CLOSE TOGETHER and each particle exerts a SMALLER PULL FORCE on every other particle.
- The particles MOVE AROUND in ANY DIRECTION within the liquid.

GASES

PARTICLES IN A GAS LOOK LIKE ...

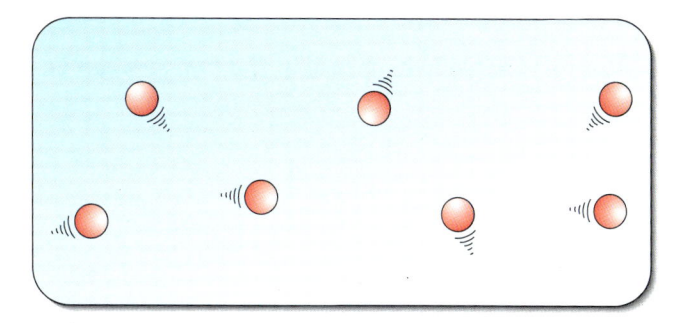

- The particles are FAR APART and there is NO PULL FORCE between them.
- The particles MOVE AROUND QUICKLY in ANY DIRECTION within their container.

EXPANSION OF SOLIDS EXPLAINED USING PARTICLE THEORY

When a solid is heated, apart from its temperature increasing it also EXPANDS (its volume becomes bigger).

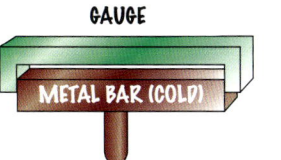

Before heating the metal bar fits in the gauge.

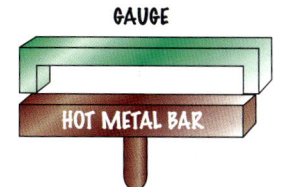

After heating the metal bar has expanded and no longer fits in the gauge.

What has actually happened to the metal bar can be explained using PARTICLE THEORY.

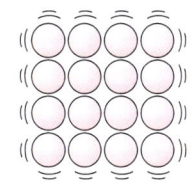

WHEN HEATED THE PARTICLES GAIN ENERGY. THEY NOW VIBRATE FASTER AND MOVE FURTHER APART. THE METAL BAR EXPANDS.

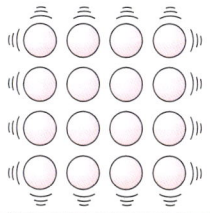

DIFFUSION

Particle Model Of Solids, Liquids And Gases

3

DIFFUSION

If you pass the school canteen when it's nearly lunch time you can't fail to smell the delicious aroma of the food being prepared. Particles of gas given off by the food spread out through the air. You can't see these particles but you can smell them. This effect is known as DIFFUSION.

- Food Particles
- Air Particles

DIFFUSION IN GASES

Diffusion in gases can be demonstrated by taking two jars of gas, one containing OXYGEN and the other BROMINE, a brownish gas. To begin with the two gases are separated from each other.

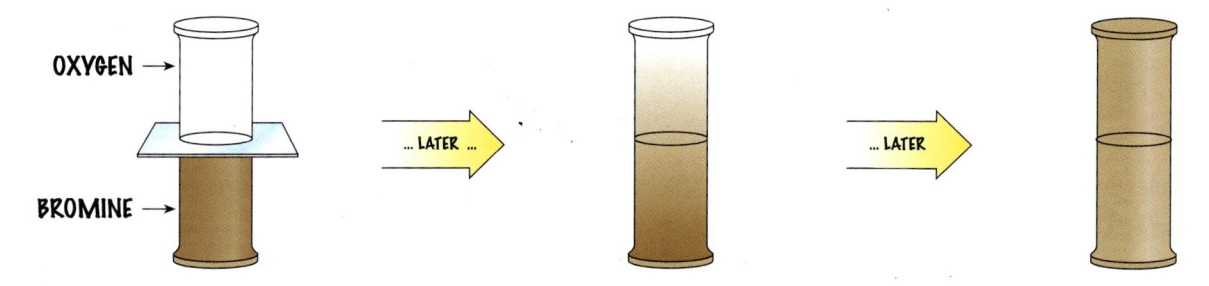

OXYGEN →
BROMINE →

... LATER ... → ... LATER →

What has actually happened in the two jars can be explained using PARTICLE THEORY.

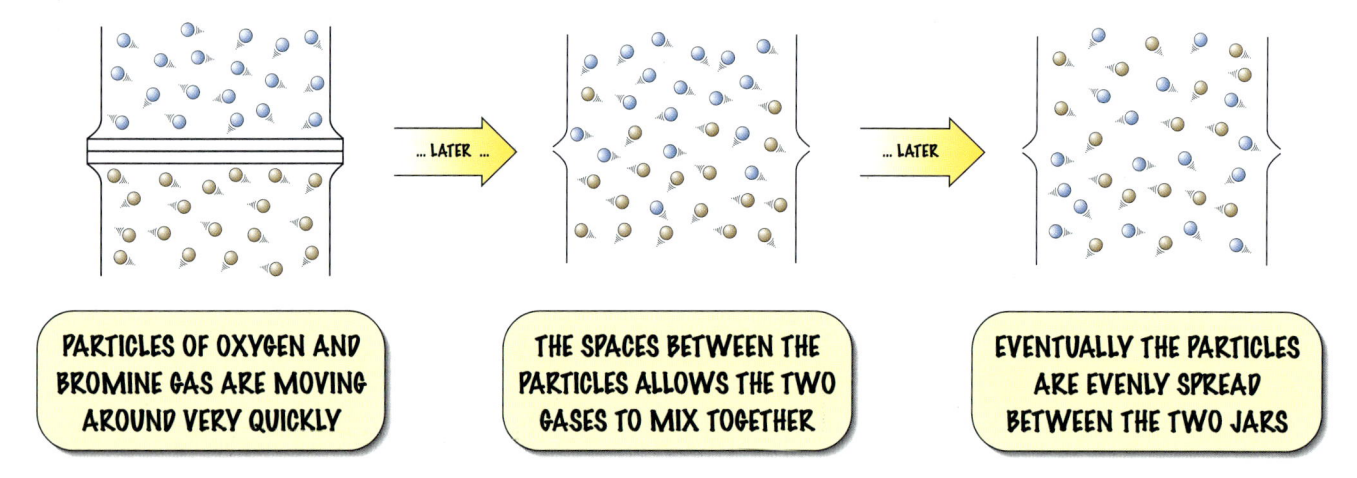

... LATER ... → ... LATER →

- PARTICLES OF OXYGEN AND BROMINE GAS ARE MOVING AROUND VERY QUICKLY
- THE SPACES BETWEEN THE PARTICLES ALLOWS THE TWO GASES TO MIX TOGETHER
- EVENTUALLY THE PARTICLES ARE EVENLY SPREAD BETWEEN THE TWO JARS

DIFFUSION IN LIQUIDS

Diffusion is also a process that occurs in liquids. The mixing together of the two liquids takes longer since liquid particles move around more slowly than gas particles.

INK →
WATER →

... LATER ... → ... LATER →

GAS PRESSURE

Particle Model Of Solids, Liquids And Gases — 4

WHAT IS GAS PRESSURE?

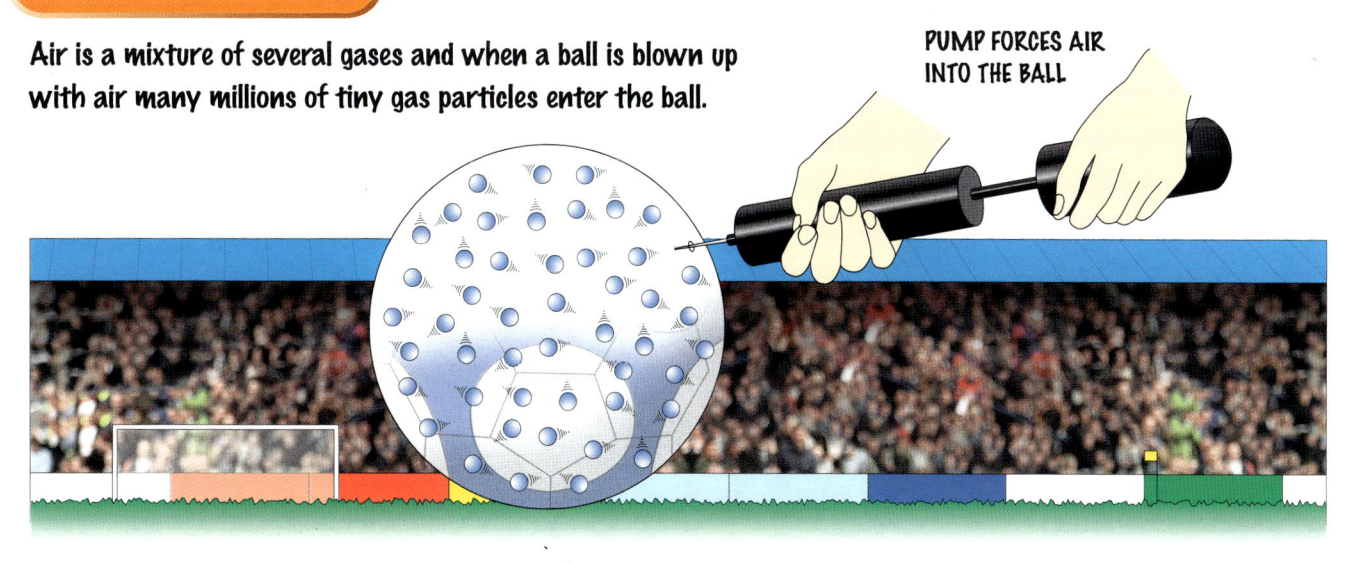

Air is a mixture of several gases and when a ball is blown up with air many millions of tiny gas particles enter the ball.

PUMP FORCES AIR INTO THE BALL

Once inside, the gas particles constantly hit the inside surface of the ball because they are moving around very quickly and in all directions. This constant hitting of the inside surface creates GAS PRESSURE.

COLLAPSING CAN EXPERIMENT

Here on earth we live at the bottom of a 'sea of air'. All around us gas particles are constantly hitting us and everything else in their way. The ball above would have gas particles constantly hitting its outside surface. As this experiment shows these gas particles can have a devastating effect if they are not opposed.

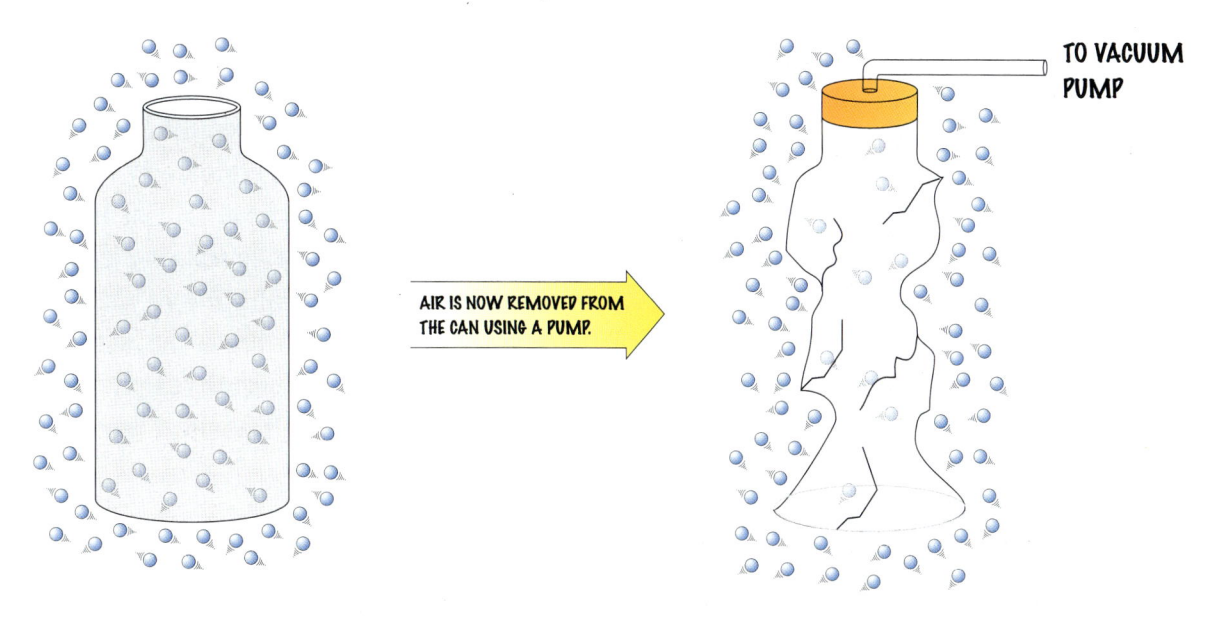

AIR IS NOW REMOVED FROM THE CAN USING A PUMP.

TO VACUUM PUMP

Normally the number of gas particles hitting the inside of the can is the SAME as the number of particles hitting the outside of the can. They cancel each other out and there is no effect on the can.

As the air inside the can is removed the number of gas particles hitting the inside of the can is LESS THAN the number of particles hitting the outside of the can. This difference causes the can to 'collapse'.

Lonsdale Science Revision Guides

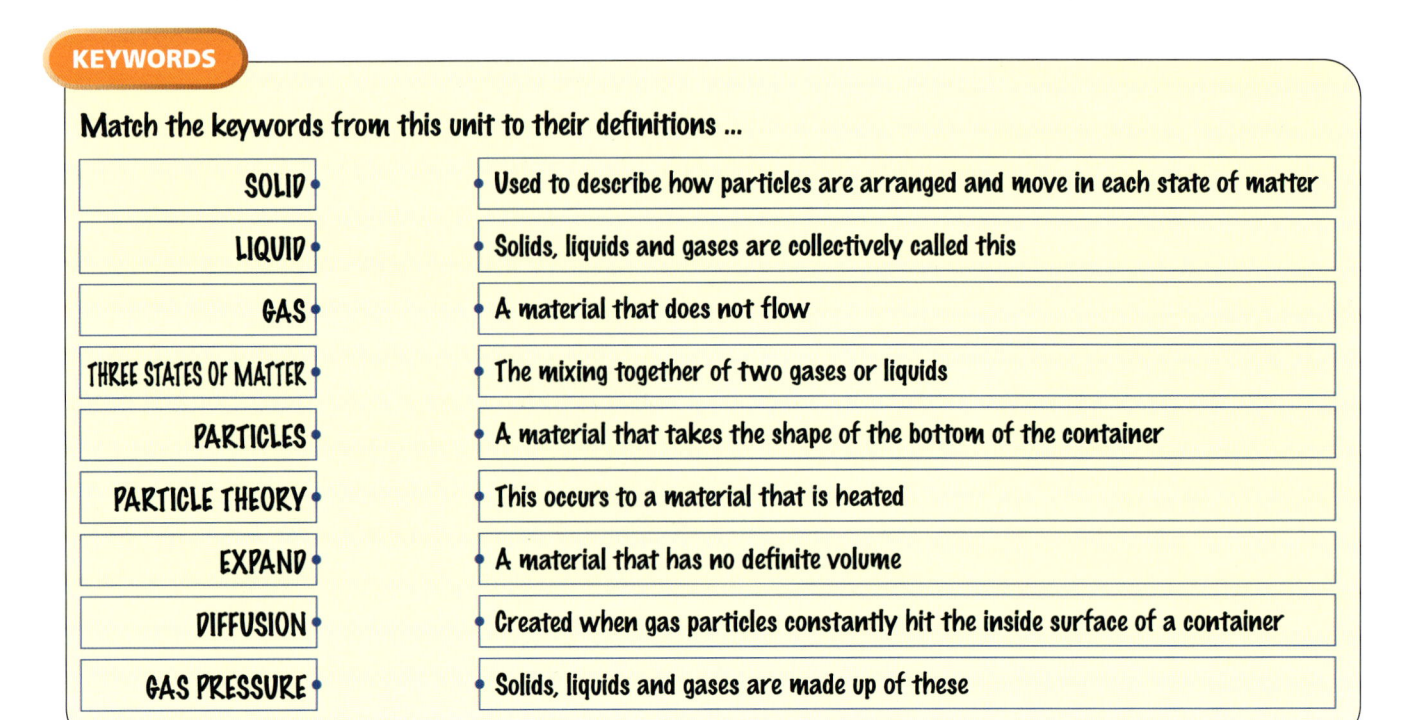

KEYWORDS AND COMPREHENSION
Particle Model Of Solids, Liquids And Gases — 5

KEYWORDS

Match the keywords from this unit to their definitions ...

SOLID	Used to describe how particles are arranged and move in each state of matter
LIQUID	Solids, liquids and gases are collectively called this
GAS	A material that does not flow
THREE STATES OF MATTER	The mixing together of two gases or liquids
PARTICLES	A material that takes the shape of the bottom of the container
PARTICLE THEORY	This occurs to a material that is heated
EXPAND	A material that has no definite volume
DIFFUSION	Created when gas particles constantly hit the inside surface of a container
GAS PRESSURE	Solids, liquids and gases are made up of these

BROWNIAN MOTION

Read this passage and then answer the questions below.

A very long time ago it was thought by the Greeks that all substances were made up of tiny particles. Unfortunately it could not be proven. In the early nineteenth century Robert Brown, a biologist, was examining some pollen grains in water using a microscope. He noticed that the pollen grains weren't still but were constantly moving around in a random haphazard way. This movement of the pollen grains became known as Brownian motion although Robert Brown himself could not explain why the pollen grains behaved in this way. Brownian motion can also be observed in smoke particles in air. This time it is the smoke particles which move around randomly. Both of these observations can be explained if liquid particles and gas particles are themselves moving around. In the case of the pollen grains the very small water particles are constantly colliding with them causing them to move around, while in the case of the smoke particles the very small air particles are constantly colliding with them causing the same effect. Both the water particles and the air particles are far too small to see, even if we use a microscope.

1. Why could the Greeks not prove that substances are made up of tiny particles?
2. What would Robert Brown have observed if he had looked at the pollen grains without a microscope?
3. Why did the pollen grains move around randomly rather than in one particular direction?
4. Do you think that Robert Brown would have observed Brownian motion if there had been the same number of pollen grains and water particles? Explain your answer.
5. When the temperature of water is increased the water particles move around more quickly. What would Robert Brown have observed if he had used water at a higher temperature?

TESTING UNDERSTANDING

Particle Model Of Solids, Liquids And Gases — 6

SOLIDS, LIQUIDS AND GASES

Solids, liquids and gases are called the .... of matter. Solids .... be compressed and they do not .... Their shape and volume stays the .... Liquids like solids cannot be .... but they do .... Their volume always stays the .... but a liquid always takes the shape of the .... of its container. Gases .... be compressed and they .... flow. A gas has no definite .... and it takes the shape of the .... it is in. The .... can be used to describe the arrangement and .... of particles. In a solid the particles are .... together and they can only .... about a fixed position. In a liquid the particles are .... together but they can move around in .... within the liquid. In a gas however the particles are .... and they move around .... in all directions.

The mixing together of two .... or two .... is known as .... The process takes longer with two .... since .... particles move around more .... compared to .... particles.

Gas pressure is created when .... particles constantly hit the .... of a container.

EXPANSION OF SOLIDS

The bar chart shows five different solids and their relative expansion when their temperature is increased by 10°C

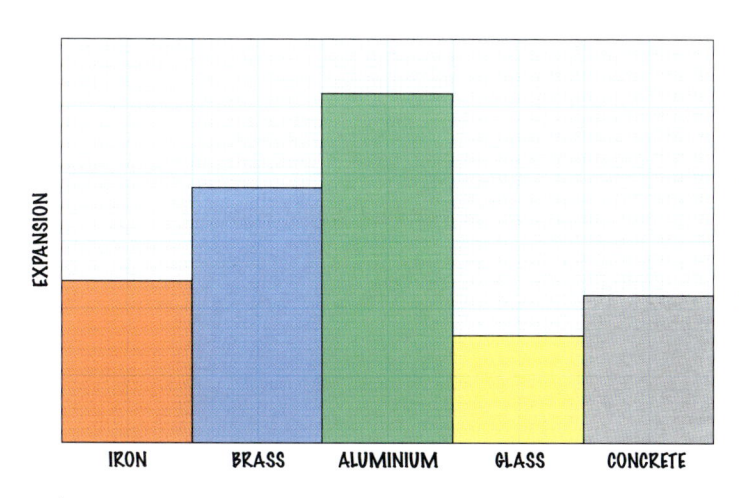

(Bar chart: IRON, BRASS, ALUMINIUM, GLASS, CONCRETE — y-axis: EXPANSION)

1. Which solid expands;
   i) the most? ....
   ii) the least? ....

2. Which two solids expand by similar amounts?
   ....

3. What would you expect to happen to each solid if their temperature is increased by another 10°C?

4. In order to be able to compare the expansion of these five solids what should all of these solids have in common before their temperature is increased?

....

SCIENTIFIC INVESTIGATION

Particle Model Of Solids, Liquids And Gases — 7

Tony was given six different materials. He was asked to investigate whether each material was a solid, a liquid or a gas. He carried out some simple tests on each material. His results are shown below although unfortunately part of his results sheet has been ripped off.

MATERIAL	CAN IT BE COMPRESSED?	DOES IT FLOW?	DOES ITS SHAPE STAY THE SAME?	DOES ITS VOLUME STAY THE SAME?
A		YES		YES
B	YES	YES		
C		NO	YES	
D	NO			
E		YES		
F	YES		YES	

1. Is material A a solid, a liquid or a gas? Explain your answer.

2. Is material B a solid, a liquid or a gas? Explain your answer.

3. Is material C a solid, a liquid or a gas? Explain your answer.

4. Tony thinks that material D is either a solid or a liquid. Which one other test would you carry out on material D to prove that it is either a solid or a liquid? Explain your choice.

5. Tony thinks that material E is either a liquid or a gas. Which one other test would you carry out on material E to prove that it is either a liquid or a gas? Explain your choice.

6. Tony thinks that material F is a liquid. Is he correct? If he is not which other test would you carry out to prove that material F is a solid or a gas.

7. If you were asked to determine the state of a particular material do you think that carrying out two tests only is sufficient? Explain your answer.

MIXING SUBSTANCES

Solutions · 1

WHAT IS A MIXTURE?

A MIXTURE is two or more substances 'jumbled up' together. Here are some common examples of mixtures.

AIR is a mixture of mainly nitrogen and oxygen.

SEA WATER is a mixture of mainly water and salt.

CRUDE OIL is a mixture of petrol, diesel, bitumen etc.

FIZZY POP is a mixture of mainly water and carbon dioxide.

SOLUTES, SOLVENTS AND SOLUTIONS

Sea water is an example of a particular type of mixture called a SOLUTION where one substance, SALT, has completely dissolved in another substance, WATER. Salt is called the SOLUTE because it dissolves in the water and water is called the SOLVENT because it does the dissolving. We can say that salt is SOLUBLE in water. Sugar is another substance that also dissolves in water.

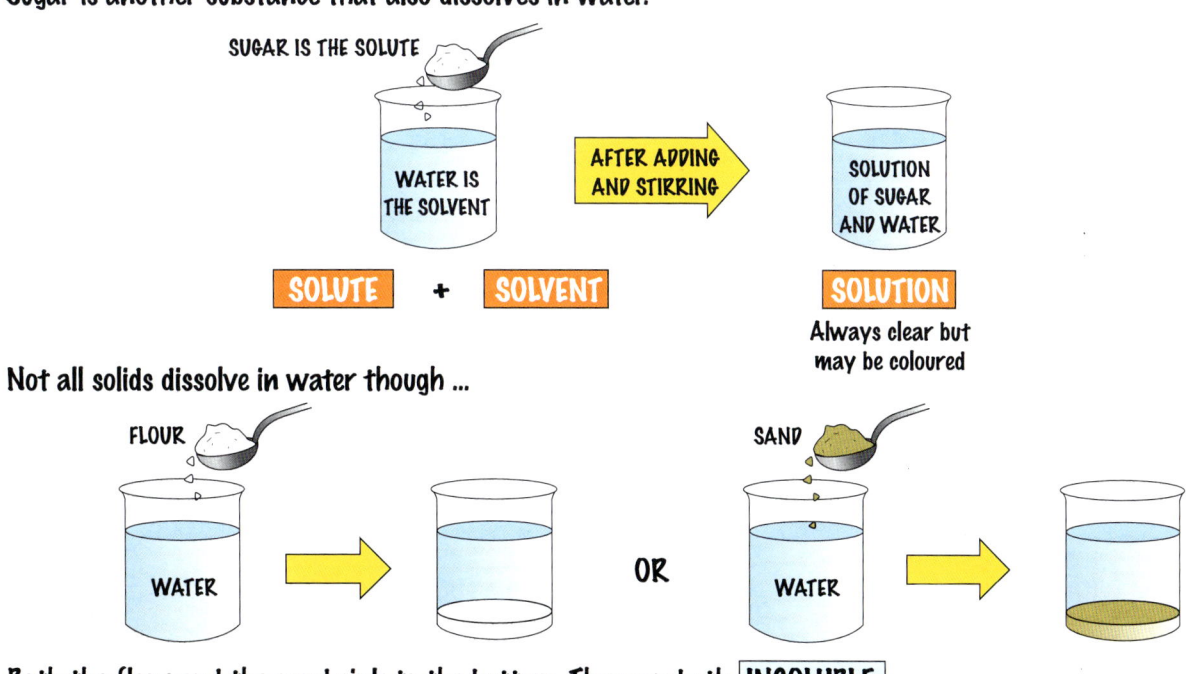

SUGAR IS THE SOLUTE
WATER IS THE SOLVENT
AFTER ADDING AND STIRRING
SOLUTION OF SUGAR AND WATER

SOLUTE + SOLVENT = SOLUTION
Always clear but may be coloured

Not all solids dissolve in water though ...

FLOUR / WATER   OR   SAND / WATER

Both the flour and the sand sink to the bottom. They are both INSOLUBLE.

WHAT HAPPENS WHEN A SOLUTE DISSOLVES

If we add 5g of sugar to 100g of water and stir, the sugar dissolves, and we get 105g of sugar solution. It may seem that the sugar has 'disappeared', but all that happens is that the sugar crystals break up into very small sugar particles, far too small for the eye to see. These sugar particles then spread out and mix completely with the water particles. We can show this using PARTICLE THEORY.

5g OF SUGAR
100g OF WATER
AFTER ADDING AND STIRRING
105g OF SUGAR SOLUTION. THE SUGAR PARTICLES (○) SPREAD OUT AND MIX COMPLETELY WITH THE WATER PARTICLES (○)

Lonsdale Science Revision Guides

DISTILLATION

Solutions 2

You will already have seen the separation of a soluble solid from a liquid when we want to COLLECT THE SOLID. More than likely you will have done this with saltwater. The solution is left in a warm place, the water evaporates away leaving behind salt crystals.

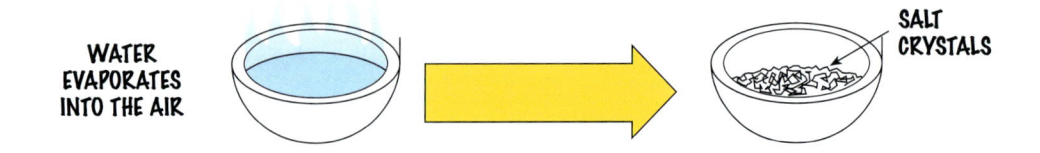

WATER EVAPORATES INTO THE AIR → SALT CRYSTALS

DISTILLATION is one step on from this. However it is still the separation of a soluble solid from a liquid, only this time we want to COLLECT THE LIQUID. Again we can use saltwater (or sea water) which can be distilled to produce pure water, which is drinkable but rather tasteless. This can be done on a small scale in the laboratory as follows:

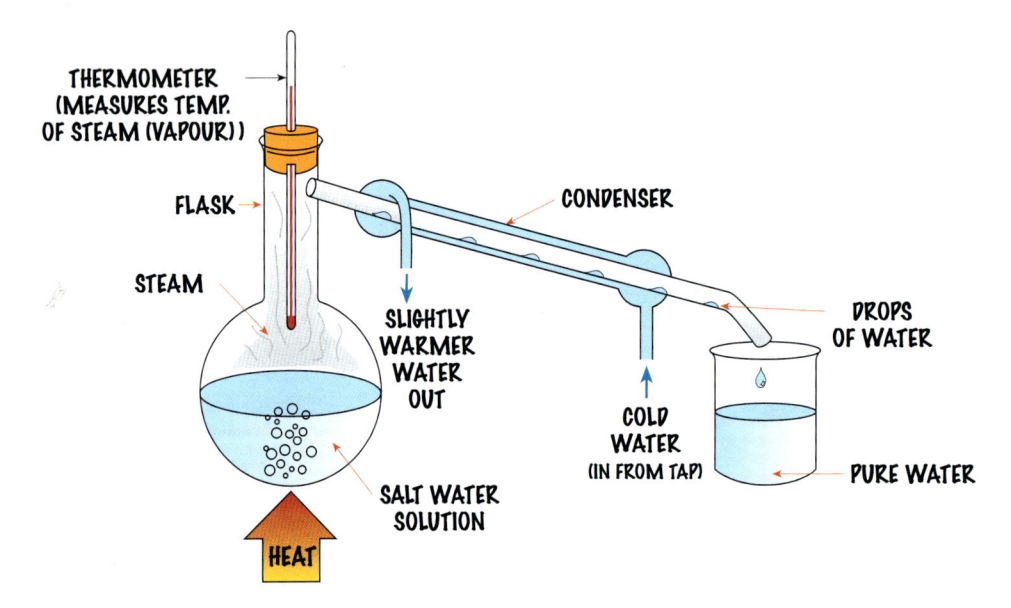

- THERMOMETER (MEASURES TEMP. OF STEAM (VAPOUR))
- FLASK
- STEAM
- CONDENSER
- SLIGHTLY WARMER WATER OUT
- DROPS OF WATER
- COLD WATER (IN FROM TAP)
- PURE WATER
- SALT WATER SOLUTION
- HEAT

Distillation involves two processes:

1. EVAPORATION

The SALT WATER solution is boiled using a bunsen burner. WATER turns to STEAM and RISES UP THE FLASK.
ALL THE SALT is left behind in the bottom of the flask.

And if we think of the particles involved ...

LIQUID PARTICLES → EVAPORATION → GAS PARTICLES

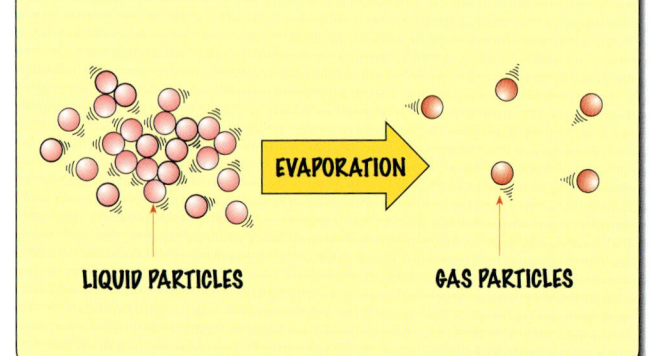

2. CONDENSATION

The STEAM (vapour) passes through the tubing and reaches the COLD SURFACE of the CONDENSER.
The steam then CONDENSES back into PURE WATER which is collected.

And if we think of the particles involved ...

GAS PARTICLES → CONDENSATION → LIQUID PARTICLES

Lonsdale Science Revision Guides

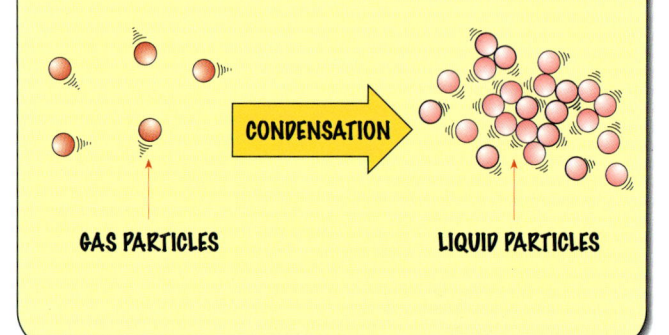

CHROMATOGRAPHY

● Solutions 3

CHROMATOGRAPHY is a method used to SEPARATE SMALL AMOUNTS of TWO or MORE SOLUTES (solids) which are SOLUBLE in a PARTICULAR SOLVENT.

If we wanted to separate the different solids (called pigments), in a particular colour of ink we could do this as follows ...

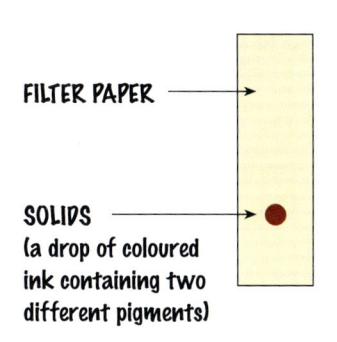

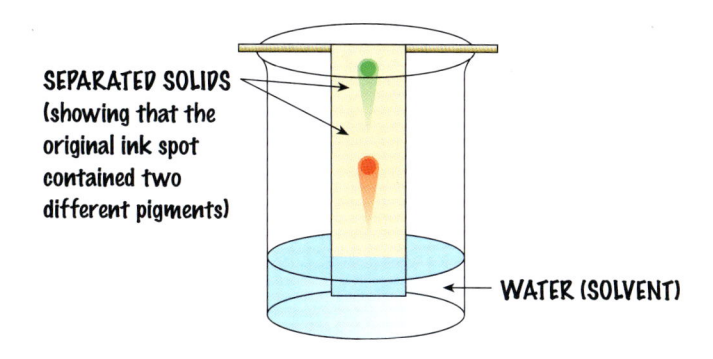

FILTER PAPER

SOLIDS (a drop of coloured ink containing two different pigments)

SEPARATED SOLIDS (showing that the original ink spot contained two different pigments)

WATER (SOLVENT)

If the mixture of pigments (solids) has not already been dissolved in water (solvent) then you will need to make up a solution. Put a concentrated drop of the solution on the FILTER PAPER.
The WATER in the solution EVAPORATES away to leave the PIGMENTS BEHIND. This can be repeated to produce a more concentrated spot.

The pigments being investigated must remain just above the water level which covers the bottom centimetre of the filter paper.
As the water rises up the paper the pigments dissolve in the water and are carried up the paper. The MORE SOLUBLE PIGMENTS TRAVEL FURTHER UP THE PAPER.
We now have a CHROMATOGRAM.

USING CHROMATOGRAMS TO IDENTIFY VARIOUS SUBSTANCES

Different substances give us different chromatograms. If we take the chromatogram of an unknown substance and compare it with chromatograms of known substances then it is possible to identify the solids that make up the unknown chromatogram.

Below is a chromatogram of the pigments contained in an unknown ink, X, and four other inks.

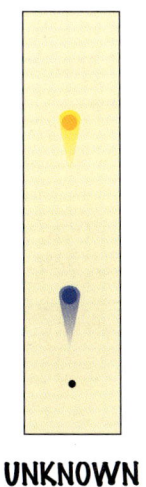

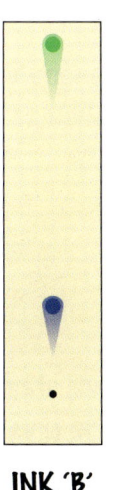

UNKNOWN INK   INK 'A'   INK 'B'   INK 'C'   INK 'D'   ← Starting Point

By comparing the chromatograms you can see that the unknown ink is ink 'D'.
This method of identifying substances using known chromatograms has many uses especially by the police in forensic science.

SATURATED SOLUTIONS

Solutions 4

If we add a solid to a liquid and the solid dissolves, the resulting mixture is called a **SOLUTION**.
If we keep on adding the solid a point is reached where the solid added no longer dissolves, no matter how long we stir, and the solid sinks to the bottom. When this happens we have a **SATURATED SOLUTION**.

A saturated solution can be made by adding instant coffee to water.

A spoonful of coffee dissolves.

Another spoonful of coffee dissolves.

Another spoonful of coffee and we have a SATURATED SOLUTION. The coffee that doesn't dissolve sinks to the bottom.

The amount or MASS of solid added is not the only factor that determines when a solution becomes saturated. Here are three others.

1. TYPE OF SOLID ADDED

The mass of solid that dissolves in a certain liquid is different for different solids.

SALT DISSOLVES IN THE WATER

LESS BATH SALTS DISSOLVE IN THE WATER

2. TYPE OF LIQUID USED

Solids dissolve better in some liquids than in others.

SALT DISSOLVES IN WATER

SALT HARDLY DISSOLVES IN ETHANOL

3. TEMPERATURE OF THE LIQUID USED

The greater the temperature of the liquid the greater the mass of solid that dissolves. **SOLUBILITY** increases with temperature.

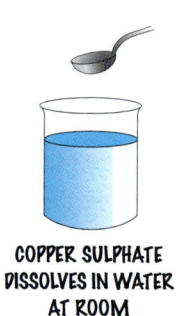

COPPER SULPHATE DISSOLVES IN WATER AT ROOM TEMPERATURE

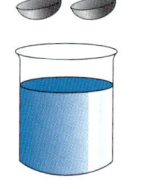

GREATER MASS OF COPPER SULPHATE DISSOLVES IN WATER AT A HIGHER TEMPERATURE

FORMING CRYSTALS FROM SOLUTIONS

One way of forming crystals of different chemicals is to make up a saturated solution and then let it cool down.
100g of water at 50°C will dissolve approximately 35g of copper sulphate to make a saturated solution.

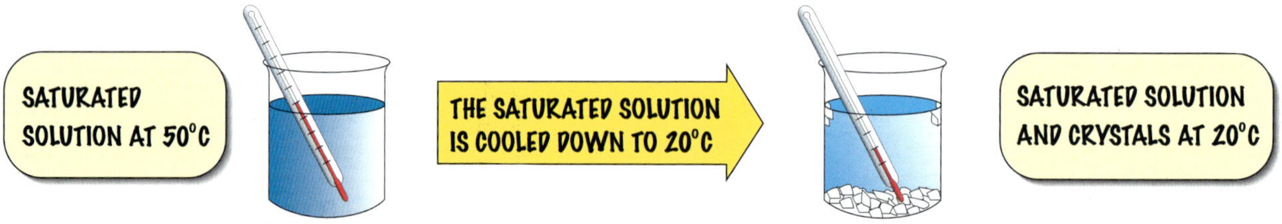

SATURATED SOLUTION AT 50°C → THE SATURATED SOLUTION IS COOLED DOWN TO 20°C → SATURATED SOLUTION AND CRYSTALS AT 20°C

As it cools down to 20°C approximately 20g of the copper sulphate will stay dissolved.
The other 15g of copper sulphate has now come out of solution to form crystals.
Cooling the solution down slowly produces the largest crystals.

Crystals can also be formed by making up a saturated solution at room temperature and then letting the water in the solution evaporate away. As the water evaporates crystals will form.

KEYWORDS AND COMPREHENSION
Solutions 5

KEYWORDS

Match the keywords from this unit to their definitions ...

MIXTURE	A solution becomes this when no more solid will dissolve in it
SOLUTE	If a solute does not dissolve in a solvent then it is....
SOLVENT	Two or more substances 'jumbled up' together
SOLUTION	Method used to separate solids that are soluble in a particular liquid
SOLUBLE	When a liquid changes into a gas
INSOLUBLE	A solid that dissolves
DISTILLATION	A liquid that does the dissolving
EVAPORATION	If a solute dissolves in a solvent then it is...
CONDENSATION	Can be used to identify an unknown substance
CHROMATOGRAPHY	Method used to separate a soluble solid from a liquid
CHROMATOGRAM	When a gas changes into a liquid
SATURATED SOLUTION	Formed when a solute completely dissolves in a solvent

EXTRACTING SALT

Read this passage and then answer the questions below.

In very hot countries salt is extracted directly from sea water. Sea water is mainly a mixture of water and sodium chloride or salt. The sea water is trapped in huge shallow pools where heat energy from the Sun evaporates away the water to leave behind the salt. This method of salt production is not used in this country. In this country salt is usually found naturally underground as deposits of rock salt. Rock salt is a mixture of salt and rock such as sandstone. Rock salt mining involves boring shafts down to the rock salt. Using cutters and explosives a mine is then worked in the rock salt in order to extract it. It is then brought to the surface where it is crushed and in this form it is used on the roads in the winter to prevent the formation of ice during very cold weather. Another method is solution mining where water is pumped down a well which has been drilled into the rock salt. The salt dissolves in the water to form salt water which is then pumped back up to the surface. The water is then evaporated to leave behind the salt.

1. What is a) the solute and b) the solvent in sea water?
2. Why is the sea water trapped in 'huge shallow' pools and not in 'small deep' pools?
3. Why do we not extract salt directly from sea water in this country?
4. What are the dangers of obtaining rock salt by mining?
5. What problems are there once a rock salt mine has been closed down?
6. What a) advantage and b) disadvantage does rock salt mining have over solution mining?

TESTING UNDERSTANDING

Solutions — 6

MIXTURES AND SOLUTIONS

Two or more substances 'jumbled up' together are called a .... A .... is a solid that dissolves in a liquid. The liquid that does the dissolving is called a .... Together they make a .... A solid that doesn't .... in a liquid is called insoluble. Distillation is the method used to separate a soluble solid from a .... when we want to collect the .... and leave behind the ....

Distillation involved two processes, firstly .... of the liquid into a .... and then .... of the .... back into a liquid.

Chromatography is the method used to separate two or more .... providing that they are .... in a particular liquid. An unknown substance can be identified if we compare its chromatogram with the chromatograms of .... substances.

If a solid is added to a liquid and a point is reached where the solid no longer .... then we now have a saturated solution. Factors that affect the formation of saturated solutions are .... of solid and liquid used, ... of solid added and .... of the liquid used. With reference to this last factor solubility .... with increasing .... of the liquid.

ROCK SALT

A local authority intends to purchase rock salt with a high salt content to use on its roads during the winter months. They have approached five suppliers who have each supplied them with a sample of their rock salt. The local authority have decided to separate the salt from the rock in order to determine what percentage of each sample is salt.

1. Describe briefly how the salt can be separated from the rock?

....
....
....
....

2. Draw a bar chart to show their results.

SUPPLIER	A	B	C	D	E
% OF SALT	23	31	8	19	38

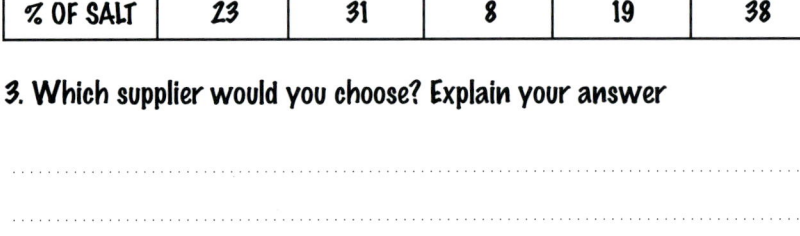

3. Which supplier would you choose? Explain your answer

....
....

58   *Lonsdale* Science Revision Guides

SCIENTIFIC INVESTIGATION

Solutions — 7

Sarah is investigating how the temperature of a liquid affects the solubility of a solid added to it. In her investigation copper sulphate crystals are dissolved in water until the solution becomes saturated. She is going to measure the mass of copper sulphate dissolved and the temperature of the water.

1. How will Sarah measure the temperature of the water?

2. Suggest one possible method that Sarah can use to measure the mass of copper sulphate dissolved.

3. What factors must Sarah keep the same in order to make this a fair test?

4. Her results are as follows:

MASS OF COPPER SULPHATE DISSOLVED (g)	22	24	28	32	30	46	58
TEMPERATURE OF WATER (°C)	20	30	40	50	60	70	80

i. On the graph paper provided plot points to show her results
ii. One of her results is obviously wrong. Ignore this result and draw a curve on your graph to pass through all the other points.

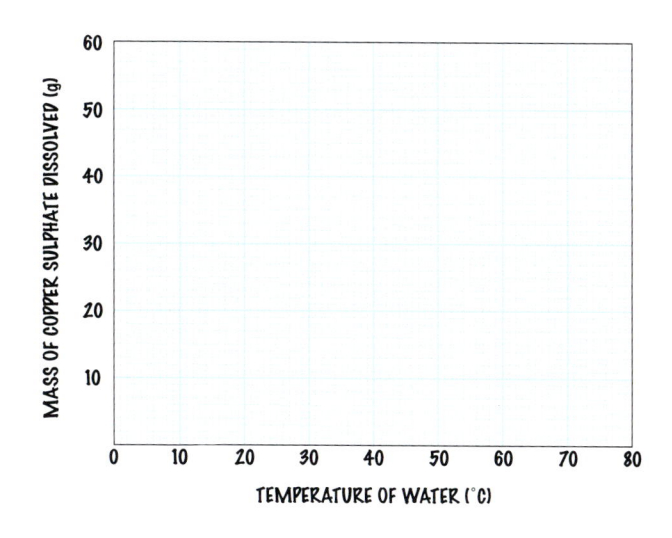

5. What conclusion can Sarah come to from her results?

6. Give as many reasons as possible why Sarah may have obtained a wrong result.

Lonsdale Science Revision Guides — 59

BURNING FUELS

● Energy Resources 1

EXAMPLES OF FUELS

A FUEL is a substance that contains ENERGY. When a fuel burns the energy is released. Some well known fuels are:

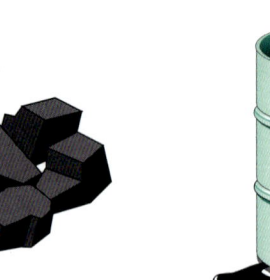

COAL   MINERAL OIL    NATURAL GAS    WOOD

When these fuels burn they release both heat and light. We can say that these fuels are sources of HEAT ENERGY and LIGHT ENERGY. A motor car uses PETROL or DIESEL as its fuel. Here the fuel is a source of MOVEMENT ENERGY.

THE BUNSEN BURNER

The BUNSEN BURNER is often used in the laboratory to burn NATURAL GAS which releases HEAT ENERGY. Whenever you use a bunsen burner it is essential that you observe the following safety rules.

BEFORE LIGHTING
- Make sure that the bunsen burner is placed near the centre of the bench.
- Place it on a heat proof mat.
- Long hair should be tied back and ties should be tucked in.
- Eye protection should be worn.
- The air hole should be closed.

TAP FULLY OPEN

ROARING FLAME WITH AIR HOLE OPEN

The size of the flame is adjusted by turning the gas tap.

The type of flame is adjusted by opening and closing the air hole.

TAP NEARLY CLOSED

YELLOW SOOTY FLAME WITH AIR HOLE CLOSED

DURING LIGHTING
- The gas is not turned on until you are ready to light the bunsen burner.
- Light at arms length using a lighted splint.

FOSSIL FUELS

Energy Resources 2

FOSSIL FUELS

COAL, MINERAL OIL and NATURAL GAS are called FOSSIL FUELS. They were formed from the 'fossilised' remains of different living organisms that died millions of years ago. The original source of these energy resources is the SUN because PLANTS store the Sun's energy and ANIMALS then eat the plants.

COAL

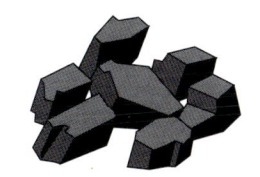

Coal was formed from the remains of DEAD TREES.

MINERAL OIL

MINERAL OIL was formed from the remains of DEAD SEA CREATURES.

NATURAL GAS

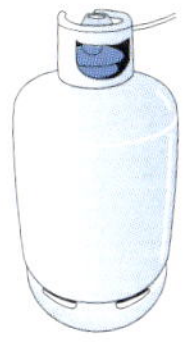

NATURAL GAS was formed from the remains of DEAD SEA CREATURES.

FOSSIL FUELS are very important substances. When they burn they release HEAT ENERGY. Power stations use this energy to produce steam which drives turbines which turn generators to produce electricity. They can also be used to produce important substances such as PLASTICS, CHEMICALS and other essential items.

Plastics   Fibres    Rubber    Cosmetics    Medicines 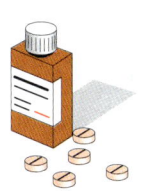   Chemicals 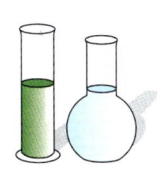   Detergents    Solvents

SAVING FOSSIL FUELS

Once a fossil fuel has been used, by being burned or changed into another substance, it cannot be used again. Because they take such a long time to form, the fossil fuels CANNOT BE REPLACED WITHIN A LIFETIME, which is why they are called NON-RENEWABLE RESOURCES. The problem this brings is that fossil fuel reserves are dwindling fast with the possibility that one or more of these fuels will run out in our lifetime. This is why there is a need to reduce the amount of fossil fuels used.

SUMMARY OF THE ADVANTAGES AND DISADVANTAGES OF FOSSIL FUELS

ADVANTAGES
- They generate a lot of energy.
- They are convenient and easy to use.

DISADVANTAGES
- They cannot be replaced within a lifetime.
- Gases are released during burning which cause damage to the environment.

RENEWABLE ENERGY RESOURCES

Energy Resources — 3

RENEWABLE ENERGY RESOURCES

WIND, WAVES, RUNNING WATER, BIOMASS, GEOTHERMAL and SUNLIGHT are all RENEWABLE ENERGY RESOURCES. Unlike the fossil fuels, they will not run out and are continuously being replaced. However as for the fossil fuels the original source of nearly all of these energy resources is the SUN.

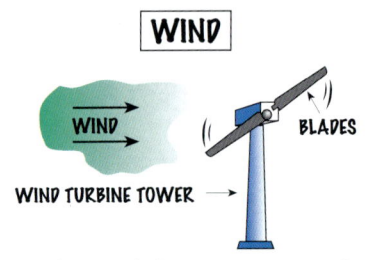

WIND
The force of the wind drives the blades of a wind turbine which turn a generator.

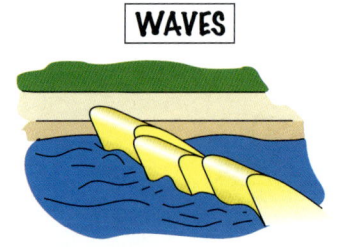

WAVES
The 'up and down' movement of the waves can be used to turn a generator.

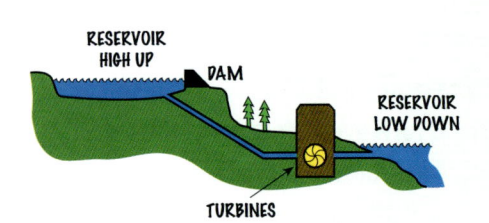

RUNNING WATER
Water stored in reservoirs flows down through pipes to drive turbines which turn generators. This is called HYDRO-ELECTRICITY.

BIOMASS
Plants and trees can be grown to provide fuel which can then be burned.

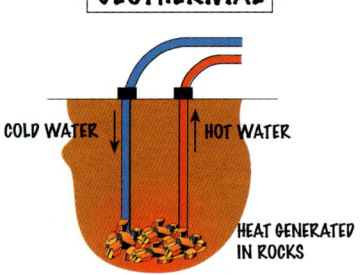

GEOTHERMAL
Some rocks under the Earth's surface are hot. Cold water pumped through these rocks becomes hotter.

SUNLIGHT
Solar cells transfer sunlight directly into electricity.

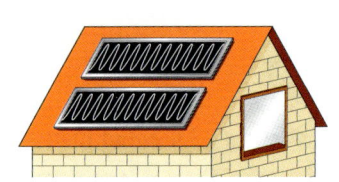

SUNLIGHT
Solar panels transfer sunlight directly into heat which is collected by water flowing through pipes.

They can be used to generate electricity or to produce heat energy and nearly all of them have the advantage that no nasty burning is involved.

SUMMARY OF THE ADVANTAGES AND DISADVANTAGES OF RENEWABLE ENERGY RESOURCES

ADVANTAGES
- They will not run out.
- They do not pollute the environment.

DISADVANTAGES
- They can be eyesore.
- The amount of energy they generate is very small compared to fossil fuels.

FOOD

Energy Resources 4

FOOD AS AN ENERGY RESOURCE

So far we have considered energy resources that release heat energy when they are burned. FOOD is also an energy resource that animals and plants need in order to live and carry out their different activities.

Different types of food contain different amounts of energy.
Energy is usually measured in JOULES although the most commonly used unit for the energy content of food is the KILOCALORIE (KCal).

BREAD
100g of bread contains 230 KCal.

MEAT
100g of lean meat contains 160 KCal.

VEGETABLES
100g of carrots contains 35KCal.

BUTTER
100g of butter contains 730 KCal.

The total number of calories a person needs to take in daily through eating or drinking depends on their age, weight, sex and activity. Too many calories or not enough will result in the weight of the person changing.

Too few calories results in a person losing weight.

Too many calories results in a person gaining weight.

WHERE DOES THE ENERGY COME FROM

Green plants need light in order to grow. In most cases, the SUN provides the energy which is then stored inside the plant as it grows. If an animal eats a plant then there is a transfer of energy from the plant to the animal. This animal could then be eaten by another animal with a further transfer of energy and so on.
A simple way to show this transfer of energy from one organism to another is to draw a FOOD CHAIN.
This always starts with the Sun as the original energy source!

Lonsdale Science Revision Guides

63

KEYWORDS AND COMPREHENSION

Energy Resources — 5

KEYWORDS

Match the keywords from this unit to their definitions ...

Keyword	Definition
FUEL	Formed from the remains of living organisms that died millions of years ago
ENERGY	Energy resource that animals need in order to live
BUNSEN BURNER	A liquid fuel that was formed from the remains of dead animals
FOSSIL FUELS	An energy resource that can be used again
COAL	Energy is usually measured in this
MINERAL OIL	Fuels release this when they burn
NATURAL GAS	Energy content of food is measured in this
NON-RENEWABLE	An energy resource that cannot be replaced in a lifetime
RENEWABLE	Substance that burns to release energy
FOOD	Used in the laboratory to burn natural gas to release heat energy
JOULES	A fuel used in the laboratory that was formed from the remains of plant and animal life
KILOCALORIE	The original source of most of the Earth's energy resources
SUN	Fuel formed from the remains of plants and trees

CRISIS, WHAT CRISIS?

Read this passage and then answer the questions below.

For a long time now there has been much talk about the need to reduce the amount of energy we use. Electrical energy is the most convenient form of energy and in this country the majority of electricity is generated in power stations using fossil fuels. Fossil fuels are the fossilised remains of living organisms which died millions of years ago. They are very precious materials since they can also be used to produce plastics and chemicals, two substances that are extremely valuable to us. If we carry on using fossil fuels at the rate we are doing then there is a distinct possibility that one or more of these fossil fuels will run out within your lifetime. One way of saving energy and the precious fossil fuels as well as saving money is to reduce heat energy losses in the home. For a typical house, fibreglass roof insulation in the loft would cost about £400, but it would save you £80 a year on your heating bill. Draught excluders cost about £40 and they save you £20 a year. Cavity wall insulation costs about £600 with £30 being saved every year and double glazing would cost about £1800 with a saving of £60 a year.

1. Why is electrical energy our most convenient form of energy?
2. What are the THREE fossil fuels?
3. Give TWO reasons why fossil fuels are likely to run out in your lifetime.
4. If you were to install fibreglass roof insulation in your home, how many years would it take before it repaid the money it cost you to install?
5. It would take you 30 years to recoup the cost of installing double glazing. Why then do home owners install double glazing?
6. Which of the above energy saving methods do you think is the most effective? Explain your answer.

TESTING UNDERSTANDING

Energy Resources 6

ENERGY

A substance that burns releasing .... energy and .... energy is called a .... In the laboratory a .... is used to burn natural gas in order to produce .... energy. The size of the flame can be changed by turning the .... and the type of flame can be changed by .... and .... the air hole.

Fuels that were formed from the fossilised remains of living organisms are called .... They can be used in power stations to produce .... and they can also be used to produce useful substances such as .... and .... When coal, mineral oil and natural gas are burned they .... be used again. Because they cannot be replaced in a lifetime they are called .... energy resources.

Energy resources that can be used again and again are called .... energy resources. They can also be used to produce .... with the advantage that there is no .... involved.

.... also need an energy resource called food in order to live. Energy is usually measured in .... However the energy content of food is measured in .... The original source of energy for nearly all the different energy resources is the ....

USES OF MINERAL OIL

The pie chart below shows the uses of mineral oil in this country.

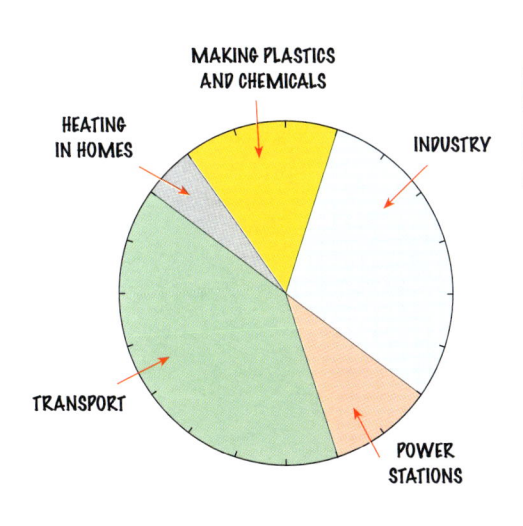

1. If each division represents 5%, complete the following table.

USE	INDUSTRY	POWER STATIONS	TRANSPORT	HEATING IN HOMES	MAKING PLASTICS AND CHEMICALS
PERCENTAGE OF MINERAL OIL USED					

2. Draw a bar graph to show the above table.

Lonsdale Science Revision Guides

SCIENTIFIC INVESTIGATION

Energy Resources — 7

You have been asked to write a plan for an investigation into the energy content of different foods by burning the foods and measuring the rise in temperature of water caused by the burning food. You have the following foods available: BREAKFAST CEREAL, CRISP BREAD, DRIED BREAD and MARSHMALLOW.

1. Give three variables that you need to control in order to make this a fair test.

   i) ....

   ii) ....

   iii) ....

2. List the apparatus you will need:

   ....

   ....

3. Draw a fully labelled diagram of your apparatus and briefly write down what you are going to do and what measurements you are going to take.

4. What safety precautions do you need to follow during this investigation?

   ....

   ....

5. Draw a table of your results, making sure that you include any units.

Lonsdale Science Revision Guides

ELECTRICAL CIRCUITS

All electrical circuits have a CELL or BATTERY which provides ELECTRIC CURRENT. If the circuit is complete, the current will flow from one end of the cell or battery through any wires, devices or components which make up the circuit and then back again to the other end of the cell or battery.

WHAT IT IS	WHAT IT LOOKS LIKE	IT'S SYMBOL	WHAT IT DOES
CELL			PROVIDES THE ELECTRIC CURRENT
BATTERY (two or more cells joined end to end)			PROVIDES THE ELECTRIC CURRENT
BULB (called a component)			PRODUCES LIGHT
SWITCH (called a device)		OPEN / CLOSED	SWITCHES THE CIRCUIT 'ON' OR 'OFF'
WIRES			ELECTRIC CURRENT FLOWS THROUGH THESE TO THE DEVICES AND COMPONENTS

DRAWING CIRCUITS

To represent a circuit using symbols all you have to do is:
- Firstly draw your cell or battery.
- Work your way round from one end of the cell or battery to the other end, drawing the symbols for all wires, devices and components as you go along. You must remember that wires are always drawn as straight lines. Both of the circuits below are examples of SERIES CIRCUITS since everything is connected together in ONE LOOP.

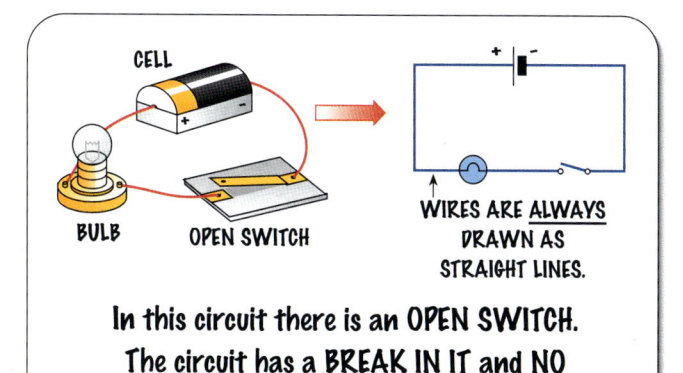

WIRES ARE ALWAYS DRAWN AS STRAIGHT LINES.

In this circuit there is an OPEN SWITCH. The circuit has a BREAK IN IT and NO CURRENT flows. The bulb is 'off'.

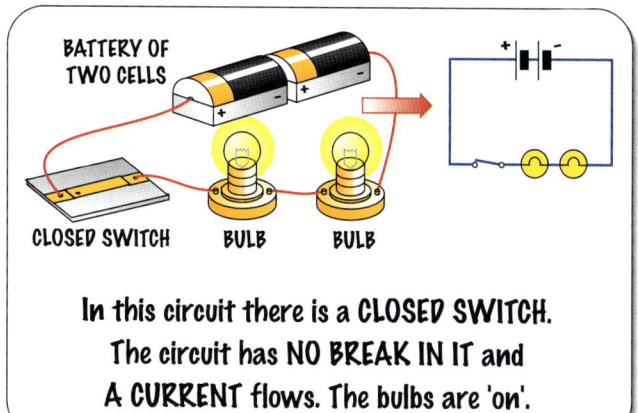

In this circuit there is a CLOSED SWITCH. The circuit has NO BREAK IN IT and A CURRENT flows. The bulbs are 'on'.

Lonsdale Science Revision Guides

ELECTRIC CURRENT

Electrical Circuits — 2

MEASURING ELECTRIC CURRENT

The ELECTRIC CURRENT that flows through a COMPLETE series circuit can be measured using an AMMETER. Electric current is measured in AMPS, (A).

In the simplest series circuit possible i.e. one cell and one bulb, the current flowing can be measured by connecting an ammeter into the circuit as shown.

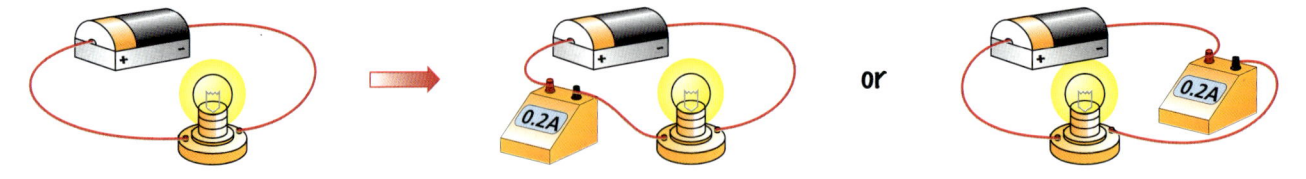

You will notice that BOTH ammeter readings are the same which shows that:
1. It doesn't matter where you position the ammeter in a series circuit.
2. Electric current does not get 'used up' by the bulb, it simply flows around the circuit.

FACTORS AFFECTING THE SIZE OF THE CURRENT

The amount of electric current that flows depends on:

1. THE NUMBER OF COMPONENTS (e.g. BULBS) IN THE CIRCUIT.

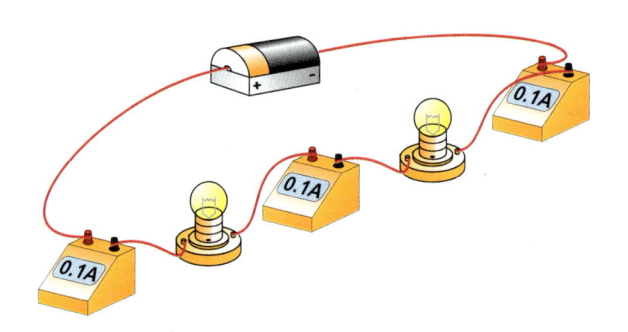

If we increase the number of bulbs in the circuit the current reading decreases. All components have RESISTANCE which means they resist the flow of electric current. Two bulbs together provide a greater resistance than one bulb resulting in a smaller current flow.

2. THE TYPE OF COMPONENTS (e.g. BULBS) IN THE CIRCUIT.

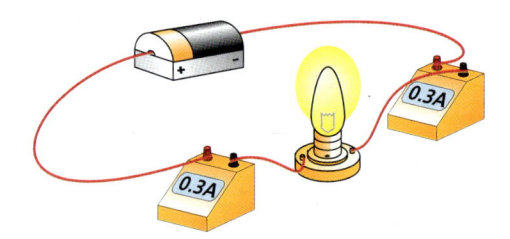

A different bulb may have a DIFFERENT RESISTANCE. This bulb has a smaller resistance resulting in a larger current flow.

3. THE NUMBER OF CELLS IN THE CIRCUIT.

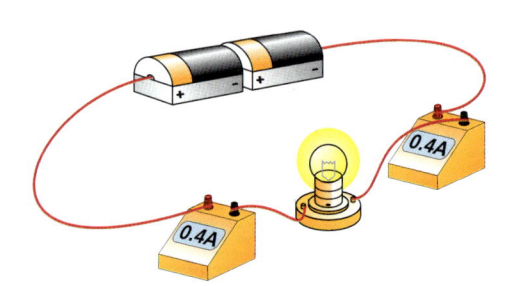

The voltage is the driving force which pushes current around the circuit. A battery of two cells provides a greater voltage which results in a larger current flow and a greater transfer of electrical energy from the battery to the bulb.

PARALLEL CIRCUITS

Electrical Circuits 3

PARALLEL CIRCUITS

In a PARALLEL CIRCUIT every component is connected separately in its own loop going from one end of the cell or battery to the other end. The simplest parallel circuit is one cell and two bulbs.

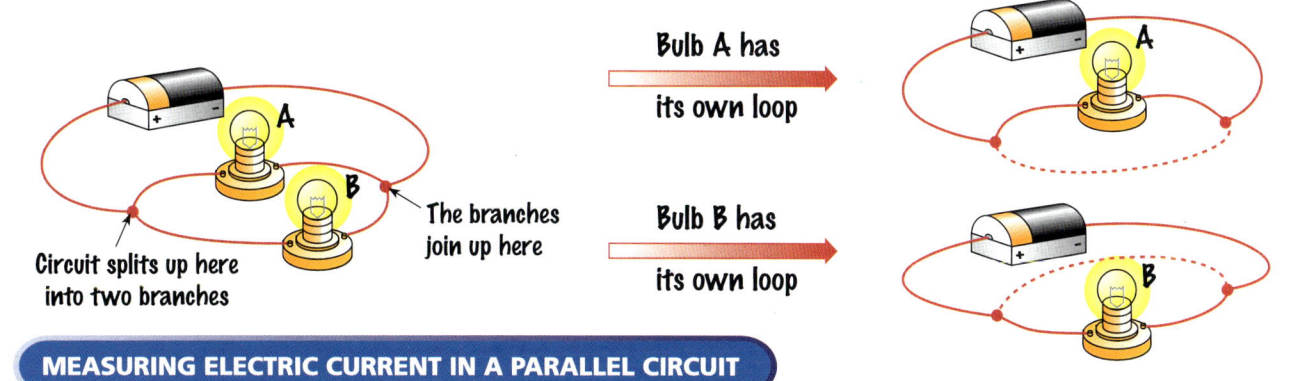

Circuit splits up here into two branches

The branches join up here

Bulb A has its own loop

Bulb B has its own loop

MEASURING ELECTRIC CURRENT IN A PARALLEL CIRCUIT

If we now include ammeters in the circuit above, and make sure that both bulbs are identical.

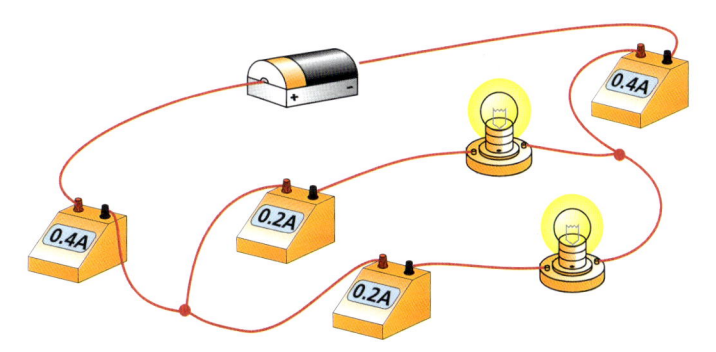

You will notice that:
1. The total current in the two branches (0.2A and 0.2A) is equal to the current in the main circuit (0.4A). Try to think of this as water flowing through a main pipe which divides into two pipes. The amount of water flowing in the main pipe is the same as the total in the two pipes added together.
2. Since the bulbs are identical the same current passes through each one and each bulb has the same brightness.

COMPARING SERIES AND PARALLEL CIRCUITS

SERIES CIRCUITS

Christmas tree lights are often connected in series. ALL THE BULBS WILL BE ON if the circuit is COMPLETE

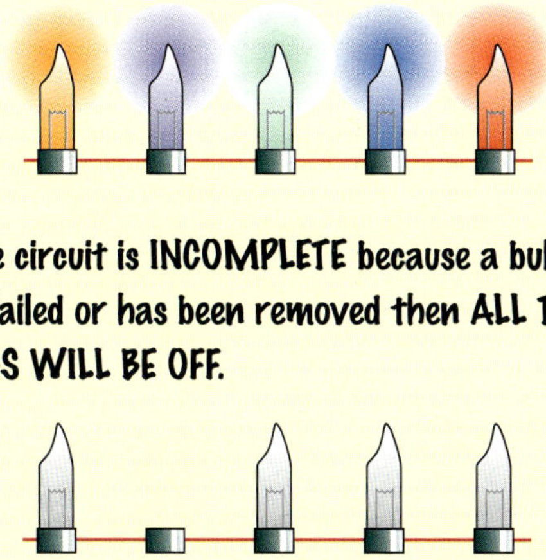

If the circuit is INCOMPLETE because a bulb has failed or has been removed then ALL THE BULBS WILL BE OFF.

PARALLEL CIRCUITS

House lights are connected in parallel. INDIVIDUAL BULBS in SEPARATE BRANCHES can be SWITCHED 'ON' or 'OFF' regardless of the other bulbs.

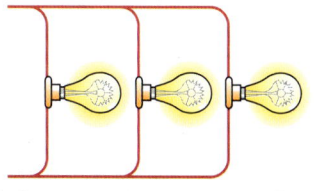

If one bulb fails, is removed, or switched off the other bulbs still work.

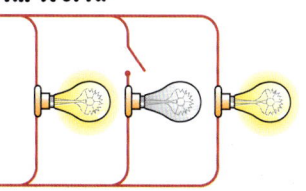

Lonsdale Science Revision Guides

DANGERS OF ELECTRICITY

Electrical Circuits 4

HOW A FUSE WORKS

When an electric current passes through a wire the electrical energy which the battery supplies is transferred by the wire into heat and light energy. If the heat produced is great enough this can cause the wire to melt and break. This is similar to how a **FUSE** is used as a safety device to protect circuits.

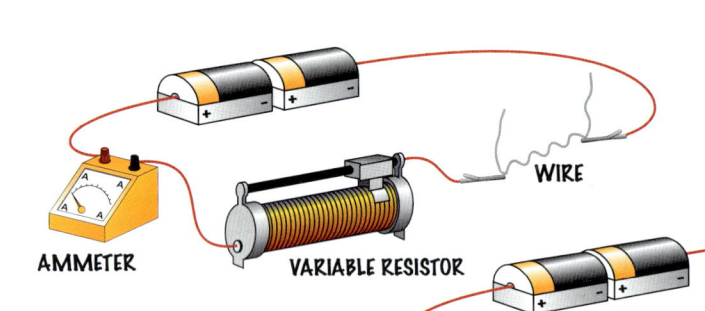

All the variable resistor does is change the current flowing in the circuit. As the current is increased the wire gets hotter and hotter, until it eventually melts and breaks, which switches the current off.

AMMETER   VARIABLE RESISTOR   WIRE

WHY DO WE NEED TO USE A FUSE

Nearly ALL ELECTRICAL APPLIANCES are connected to the mains electricity supply using a CABLE and **PLUG**.
Inside the plug there is a fuse which forms part of the wire that carries the electric current.
If a fault occurs resulting in a surge of electric current greater than normal, the wire inside the fuse will heat up, melt and break. This prevents the APPLIANCE or its CABLE from being damaged through the possibility of OVERHEATING.

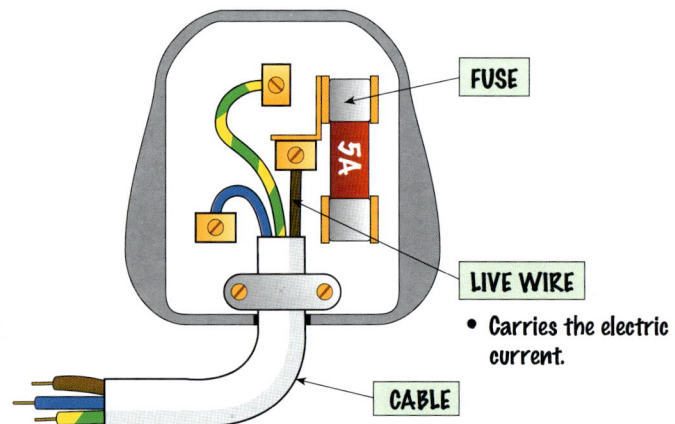

FUSE 5A

LIVE WIRE
- Carries the electric current.

CABLE

EFFECT OF ELECTRIC CURRENT ON THE BODY

The NERVES carry electrical impulses around the body. Large electric currents can cause damage to the nerves and can also cause muscles to go into 'spasm' particularly if the person remains in contact with the electric current. This can lead to heart failure with severe burns at the point where the electric current enters or leaves the body. You should also remember that the cells and batteries you use in the laboratory deliver much less energy than the MAINS SUPPLY which you use without a second thought ...

... so remember treat mains electricity with respect!

KEYWORDS AND COMPREHENSION

Electrical Circuits — 5

KEYWORDS

Match the keywords from this unit to their definitions ...

ELECTRIC CURRENT	Allows electric current to flow through them to devices and components
CELL	Two or more cells joined together
BATTERY	A safety device that melts and breaks when too big a current flows through it
BULB	A device that enables a circuit to be 'on' or 'off'
SWITCH	Electrical appliances are connected to the mains electricity through this
WIRE	This flows around a complete electrical circuit
SERIES CIRCUIT	Used to measure electric current
AMMETER	A circuit where every component is connected separately in its own loop
RESISTANCE	A component that produces light
PARALLEL CIRCUIT	Components have this to resist the flow of electric current
FUSE	Provides the electric current
PLUG	A circuit where everything is connected together in one loop

THE DEVELOPMENT OF THE BATTERY

Read this passage and then answer the questions below.

Over 200 years ago the Italian Luigi Galvani was doing some experiments using dissected frogs legs. He discovered that if the foot and the exposed nerves at the top of the leg were connected by one length of wire, half of which was made of one metal while the other half was made of another, the leg 'twitched.' What Galvani didn't realise was that he had stumbled upon the very first primitive battery and the 'twitching' had been due to a flow of electric current. Alessandro Volta, a fellow Italian, heard of Galvani's experiment and as a result carried out his own experiments, firstly using two different metals placed apart in a solution of saltwater. This arrangement was capable of producing an electric current.

One step further was the voltaic pile where copper and zinc discs were alternated one after another in a pile, separated from each other by pieces of cloth soaked in saltwater.

This voltaic cell was capable of producing a steady supply of electric current. During the 1860's Georges Leclanche, a Frenchman, was responsible for the development of the dry cell which was the forerunner to the cells and batteries we use today for many of our electrical appliances.

1. What did Galvani discover?
2. What had he stumbled upon?
3. Describe Volta's first arrangement of a battery.
4. What was the voltaic 'cell'?
5. Why was the voltaic 'cell' better than the previous arrangement?
6. Who was responsible for the development of the dry cell?
7. Why was this development important for us today?

Lonsdale Science Revision Guides

TESTING UNDERSTANDING

Electrical Circuits — 6

ELECTRICAL CIRCUITS

An electric circuit usually consists of a cell or a .... to provide the electric .... A bulb is a .... which produces .... while a switch is a .... that enables a circuit to be on or off. If all of these are connected together in one loop then we have a .... circuit. The current through a complete circuit can be measured using an .... In a .... circuit the current is the same everywhere in the circuit. The amount of electric current that flows can be changed by altering either the .... or type of components in the circuit. Another way is to change the number of .... we have. If every component is connected separately in its own loop then we have a .... circuit. In this circuit the .... divides up and is not the same everywhere in the ....

A fuse is a .... device. It forms part of the wire that carries the electric .... When the .... gets too big the fuse wire heats up causing it to .... and .... This saves both the .... and its cable from possibly being damaged by ....

FUSES

Fuses come in all shapes and sizes. Ideally the size of a fuse in Amps should be just greater than the maximum current in Amps that should normally pass through the wire? Below is a bar graph showing five different fuses and their sizes.

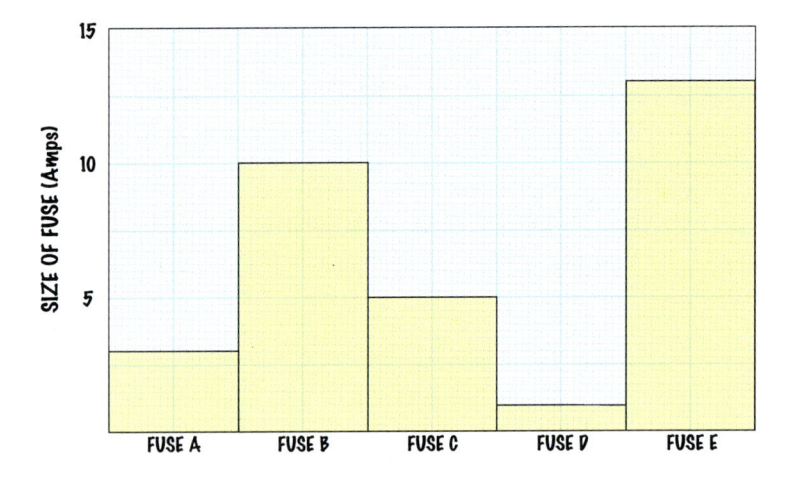

1. Which fuse should be used when the normal maximum current is ...

   i) 1.5 Amps ....

   ii) 4.9 Amps ....

   iii) 5.1 Amps ....

   iv) 11.4 Amps ....

   v) 0.3 Amps ....

2. Explain what would happen if a current greater than 5 Amps passed through a 5 Amp fuse.

SCIENTIFIC INVESTIGATION

Electrical Circuits — 7

Mary and Joe were going to investigate how the current in a series circuit depended on the number of components in the circuit. They were given six identical components, a battery of two cells and wires.

1. Which other piece of equipment would they need to complete their investigation? Explain your choice.

　..

2. They firstly connected one component in series and then two, three, five and finally six components. Each time they measured the electric current flowing in the circuit. Their results were as follows.

No. Of Components	1	2	3	5	6
Current Flowing (Amps)	1.2	0.6	0.4	0.25	0.2

　i) On the graph paper provided plot points to show their results.

　ii) Draw a curve on your graph that passes through all the points.

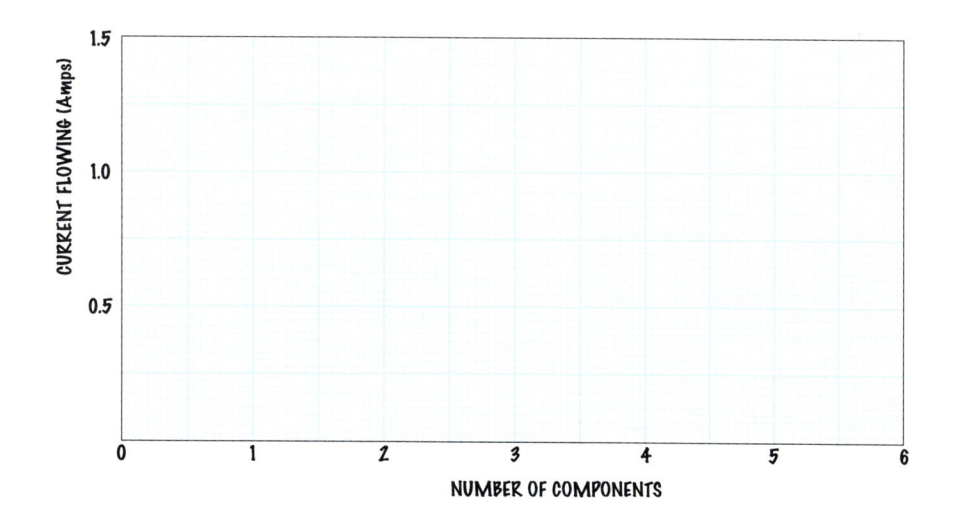

3. Use your graph to estimate the current flowing if they had connected four components in series.

　..

4. Mary thinks that the reason the current decreases when the number of components increases is because of the position of the piece of equipment in question 1 above. Is she right or wrong? Explain your answer.

　..

5. Joe, however thinks that the reason the current decreases when the number of components increases is because each component resists the flow of electric current and the more components there is the greater the resistance. Is he right or wrong? Explain your answer.

　..

FORCE, MASS AND WEIGHT

Forces And Their Effects 1

FORCES

A FORCE is a PUSH or a PULL. They are measured in NEWTONS (N). A force is drawn as a straight line with an arrow drawn at the end. The arrow shows the direction in which the force is acting.

Here are some typical forces in action.

A force called FRICTION acts against the moving cyclist.

A force called AIR RESISTANCE or DRAG acts against the falling skydiver.

A force called WEIGHT acts on the stationary girl.

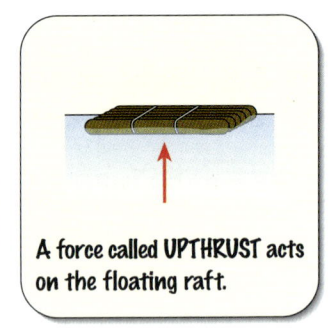

A force called UPTHRUST acts on the floating raft.

In reality forces always act in pairs. All the examples above have another force acting in the opposite direction, which, to keep it simple, we've not drawn.

BALANCED FORCES

Any object that is STATIONARY always has two EQUAL and OPPOSITE forces acting on it, ONE UPWARDS and the OTHER DOWNWARDS. We say that the forces acting are BALANCED.

The ground exerts an upward force on the girl. This force and her weight are balanced forces.

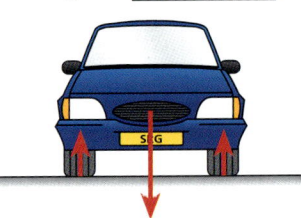

The ground exerts an upward force on the car. This force and the weight of the car are balanced forces.

MASS AND WEIGHT

The MASS of an object is the amount of matter that it contains. Mass is measured in KILOGRAMS or GRAMS. The WEIGHT of an object is the PULL FORCE that acts on the object because of GRAVITY. Since weight is a force it is measured in NEWTONS (N). The weight of an object can be measured using a FORCEMETER.

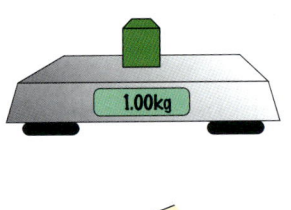

This object has a MASS of 1Kg

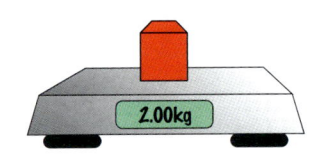

This object has a MASS of 2Kg

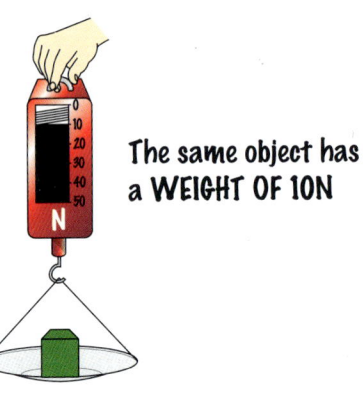

The same object has a WEIGHT OF 10N

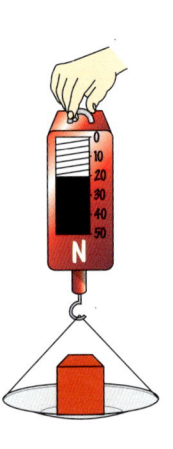

The same object has a WEIGHT OF 20N

You should notice that the weight of an object (in Newtons) is always numerically TEN TIMES BIGGER than the mass of the object (in Kilograms). On Earth this relationship between weight and mass is always true.

UPTHRUST

Forces And Their Effects — 2

UPTHRUST IN ACTION

All objects that are immersed in water experience an UPWARD FORCE from the water. This upward force is called **UPTHRUST.** You will have felt this force in action every time you've been in a swimming pool.

Two solid objects of the SAME WEIGHT, but DIFFERENT VOLUMES, are each suspended using a forcemeter. Each object is then lowered into a container of water, one sinks but the other doesn't.

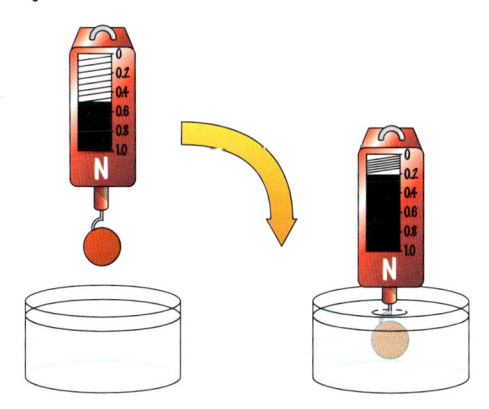

This object SINKS and the forcemeter shows that the OBJECT WEIGHS LESS IN WATER THAN IN AIR. This is true of all objects that sink, and is due to the upthrust the object is experiencing 'cancelling out' SOME of the weight of the object i.e. weight is greater than upthrust.

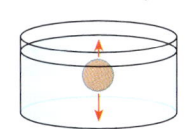

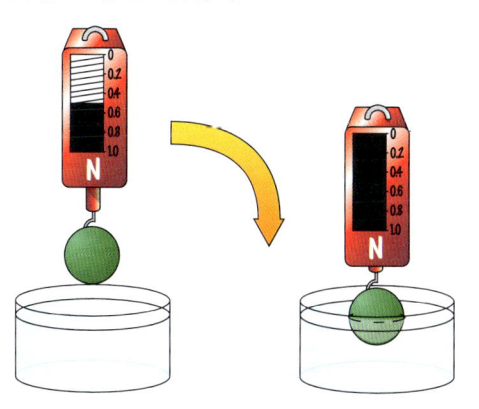

This object FLOATS and the forcemeter shows a ZERO WEIGHT READING FOR THE OBJECT. This is true for all objects that float, and is due to the upthrust the object is experiencing 'cancelling out' ALL of the weight of the object i.e. weight is equal to upthrust.

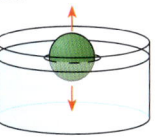

WHY DO OBJECTS FLOAT?

Any object will float in water if its **DENSITY** is less than the density of water. Denser liquids produce more upthrust. Density is a measure of how much mass of an object there is in a given volume. To calculate the density of any object we need to know its MASS and VOLUME and then we can use this formula.

$$\text{DENSITY} = \frac{\text{MASS}}{\text{VOLUME}}$$

Density is usually measured in g/cm³ (grams per centimetre cubed) and water has a density of 1 g/cm³.

EXAMPLE

The RED object above has a mass of 50g and a volume of 25cm³. The GREEN object above has a mass of 50g and a volume of 100cm³ (since both objects have the same mass they also have the same weight). Calculate the density of each object.

For the RED object:

$$\text{DENSITY} = \frac{\text{MASS}}{\text{VOLUME}} = \frac{50g}{25cm^3} = \boxed{2g/cm^3}$$

Now you know why the red object sinks as its density is more than the density of water.

For the GREEN object:

$$\text{DENSITY} = \frac{\text{MASS}}{\text{VOLUME}} = \frac{50g}{100cm^3} = \boxed{0.5g/cm^3}$$

Now you know why the green object floats as its density is less than the density of water.

FRICTION

Forces And Their Effects — 3

FRICTION is a force that resists the movement of an object. It always acts in an opposite direction to the direction the object is moving or attempting to move in. The amount of friction which is created depends on the two surfaces.

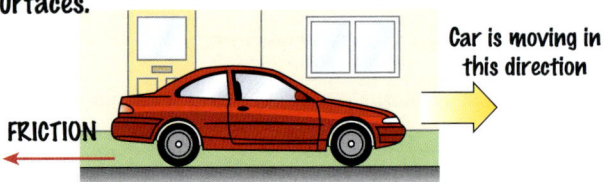

A large force of friction is created between the tyres and the road to enable the car to move.

A small force of friction is created between the skis and the snow to enable the skier to move.

REDUCING FRICTION BETWEEN SURFACES

However smooth a surface looks and feels under a microscope it would look rough and uneven. When two surfaces move past each other this roughness and unevenness causes one surface to catch on the other. This causes friction. A simple way to reduce the amount of friction is to separate the two surfaces with a LUBRICANT. Typical lubricants are oil and water.

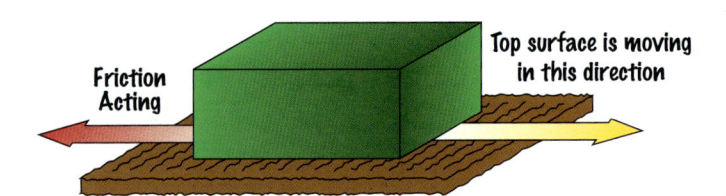

Both surfaces are rough and uneven and the amount of friction created is large.

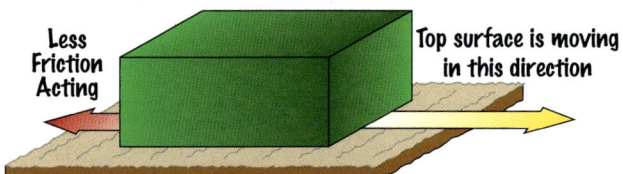

Lubricant acts to 'smooth out' the two rough surfaces and reduce the amount of friction created.

USEFUL AND UNHELPFUL FRICTION

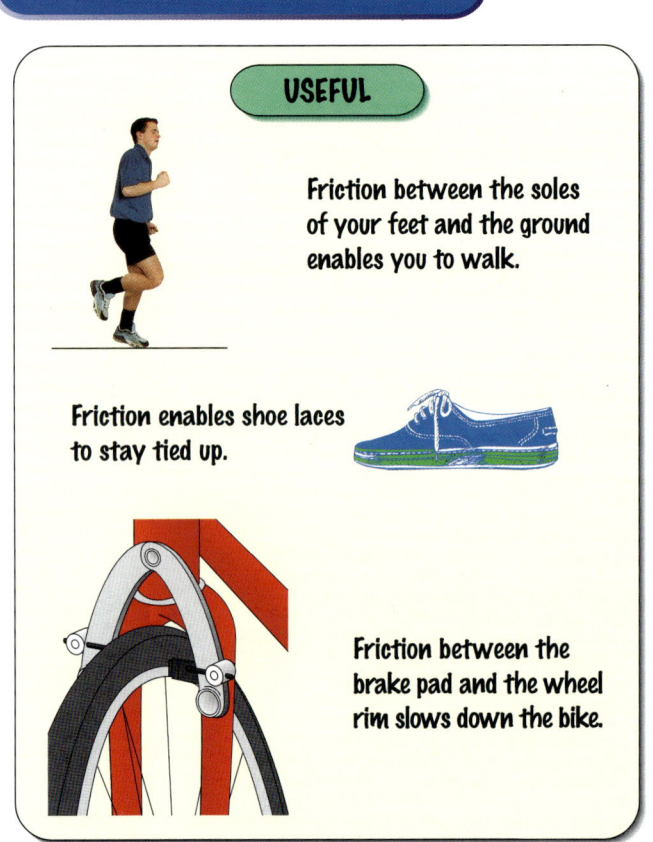

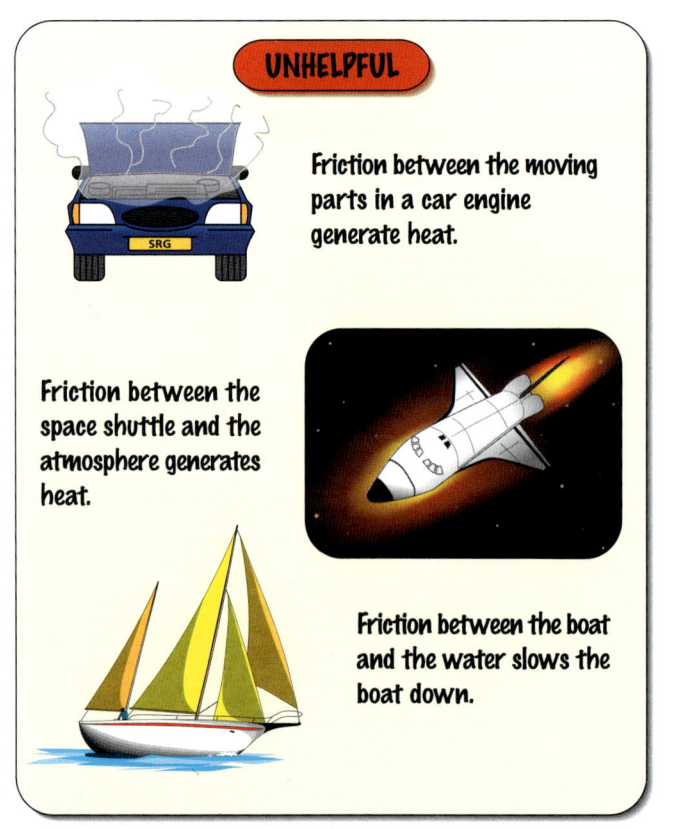

USEFUL

Friction between the soles of your feet and the ground enables you to walk.

Friction enables shoe laces to stay tied up.

Friction between the brake pad and the wheel rim slows down the bike.

UNHELPFUL

Friction between the moving parts in a car engine generate heat.

Friction between the space shuttle and the atmosphere generates heat.

Friction between the boat and the water slows the boat down.

Lonsdale Science Revision Guides

STOPPING DISTANCE OF VEHICLES

Forces And Their Effects — 4

STOPPING DISTANCE

The **STOPPING DISTANCE** of a vehicle is the distance travelled by the vehicle in coming to an emergency stop. Stopping distance includes the distance travelled while the driver is reacting and the distance travelled after the brakes are applied.

FACTORS THAT AFFECT STOPPING DISTANCE

1) THE GREATER THE SPEED OF THE VEHICLE, THE GREATER THE STOPPING DISTANCE

Speed is a measure of how fast the vehicle is moving. A vehicle travelling at 50mph (miles per hour) would travel a distance of 50 miles in 1 hour if it carried on travelling at this speed and so on. Vehicle speedometers also measure speed in km/h (kilometres per hour).

At 50mph the stopping distance is about 50m, equal to half the length of a football pitch.

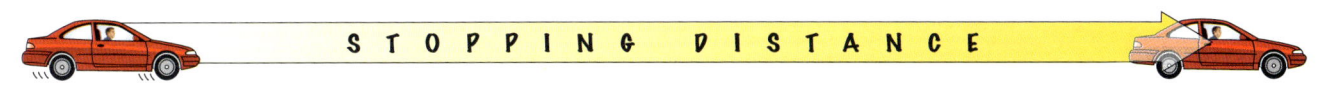

At 70mph the stopping distance is about 100m, equal to the length of a football pitch.

2) THE LESS FRICTION BETWEEN THE TYRES AND THE ROAD, THE GREATER THE STOPPING DISTANCE

When the driver applies the brakes, friction between the tyres and the road causes the vehicle to come to a stop. WET or GREASY roads reduce the amount of friction acting between the tyres and the road.

On a dry road at 50mph the stopping distance is about 50m.

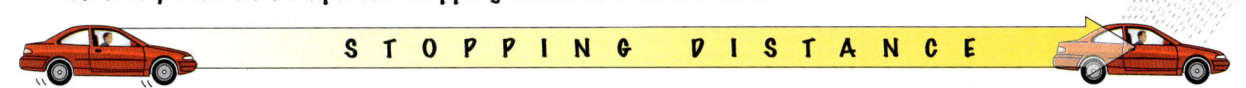

On a wet or greasy road at 50mph the stopping distance is about 80m.

DISTANCE - TIME GRAPHS

One way of describing the motion of an object is to draw a **DISTANCE-TIME GRAPH.** Here is a typical distance-time graph of a journey to school where a pupil firstly walks to a bus stop, waits for the bus and then catches a bus to school.

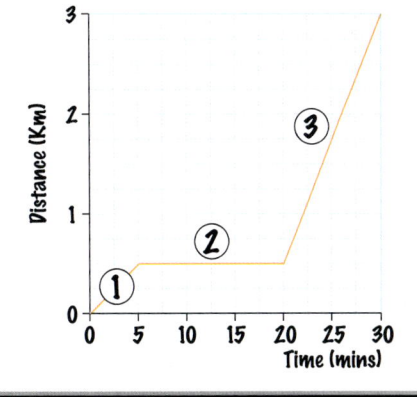

① **WALK TO THE BUS STOP**
The pupil takes 5 minutes to walk 0.5Km

② **WAIT AT THE BUS STOP**
The pupil waits 15 minutes for the bus to arrive

③ **BUS RIDE TO SCHOOL**
The bus takes 10 minutes to drive 2.5Km

Lonsdale Science Revision Guides

KEYWORDS AND COMPREHENSION

Forces And Their Effects — 5

KEYWORDS

Match the keywords from this unit to their definitions ...

FORCE	The amount of matter that an object contains measured in kilograms
NEWTONS	The distance travelled by a vehicle in coming to an emergency stop
AIR RESISTANCE	Upward force experienced by an object immersed in water
BALANCED FORCES	The units of measurement for 'Force'
MASS	This force resists the movement of an object
WEIGHT	This is used to measure the weight of an object
FORCEMETER	The motion of an object can be described by this
UPTHRUST	A push or a pull
DENSITY	Also known as drag this force acts against a falling object
FRICTION	Calculated by dividing the mass of an object by its volume
LUBRICANT	Equal and opposite forces acting on an object
STOPPING DISTANCE	Can be used to reduce the amount of friction between two surfaces
DISTANCE - TIME GRAPH	The pull force that acts on an object due to gravity

ARCHIMEDES

Read this passage and then answer the questions below.

Archimedes is perhaps the most famous scientist of ancient Greece. Born in approximately 300 B.C. he was a brilliant mathematician and inventor. A very famous legend concerns the crown of King Hieron who doubted whether his crown was made of pure gold. This presented Archimedes with a problem because to compare the 'gold' crown with pure gold he needed to know its volume. If he knew its volume he could then compare its mass with the mass of an equal volume of pure gold. If they were different then the crown wasn't 100% gold.

One day as Archimedes lowered himself into a very full bath the water overflowed. He immediately realised that this volume of water was equal to the volume of his body. In his excitement he ran naked through the streets shouted "Eureka, Eureka" which translates as 'I have found it'.

Now that Archimedes could determine the volume of the crown he worked out that the crown was not pure gold. Unfortunately for the goldsmith who had made the crown it was not a happy ending. He was executed.

1. Why couldn't Archimedes work out the volume of the crown by taking measurements with a ruler?

2. If the king had been tricked, what difference would there be between the mass of the crown and the mass of an equal volume of gold?

3. What did Archimedes need to know to work out the density of any substance?

4. Does the size of the bath into which an object is placed affect the amount of water which overflows?

5. What difficulty could there be in trying to measure the volume of an object by Archimedes' method?

TESTING UNDERSTANDING

Forces And Their Effects — 6

FORCES IN ACTION

A force that acts against a falling object is called .... or drag. Forces always act in .... and when these two forces are equal and opposite the forces acting are said to be ....

The amount of matter that an object contains is called its .... and is measured in ....

The pull force on an object due to gravity is called .... and is measured in ....

Upthrust is an .... force that acts on an object that is immersed in .... If the object floats then the upthrust is equal to the .... of the object. The density of an object depends on its .... and its .... A floating object will have a density .... than that of water while an object that sinks has a density .... than that of water.

The force that resists the movement of an object is called .... The amount of this force that acts between two surfaces can be reduced by using a ....

The stopping distance of a vehicle depends on its .... and the amount of .... between its tyres and the road. The motion of an object can be usefully described by means of a .... graph.

STOPPING DISTANCE

The table below gives the stopping distance on a dry road surface for a particular vehicle when it is travelling at a certain speed.

STOPPING DISTANCE (m)	12	22	35	51	70	92
SPEED (mph)	20	30	40	50	60	70

1. On the axes given draw a bar graph to show the data.

2. What happens to the stopping distance as the speed of the vehicle increases?

3. What would happen to the stopping distance at any particular speed if the road surface was wet? Explain your answer?

4. Name one other factor that will also change the stopping distance at any particular speed.

Lonsdale Science Revision Guides

SCIENTIFIC INVESTIGATION

Forces And Their Effects — 7

Jenny is investigating how the position of a floating object changes in water of varying salinity (saltiness). A graduated straw with a piece of plasticine stuck to one end is placed in water and the water level position is marked. She then added salt to the water, and stirred it before taking a measurement of the distance the straw moved from the original water position.

She then repeated the procedure by adding more salt. Her results are as follows:

MASS OF SALT ADDED (g)	5	10	15	20	25	30
DISTANCE STRAW MOVES (mm)	2	3	6	8	11	12

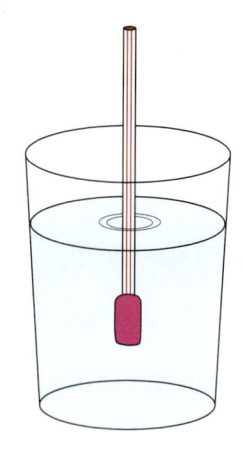

1. What factors must she keep the same in order to make this a fair test?

2. When Jenny adds the salt, why does she stir the mixture?

3. On the graph paper provided draw a line graph of her results.

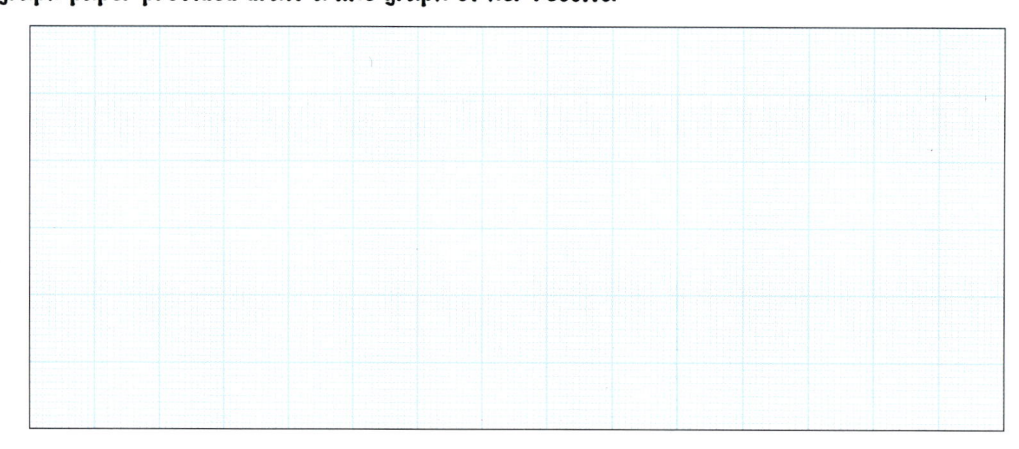

4. What conclusion does Jenny form from her results?

5. Explain using the words 'density' and 'upthrust' Jenny's conclusion.

6. Explain what would happen if the straw was immersed in a liquid whose density was less than that of water.

80

Lonsdale Science Revision Guides

THE EARTH AND THE SUN

The Solar System And Beyond — 1

THE EARTH

The EARTH rotates on a TILTED AXIS, just like a spinning top, completing one rotation every 24 HOURS giving us DAYTIME and NIGHT-TIME.

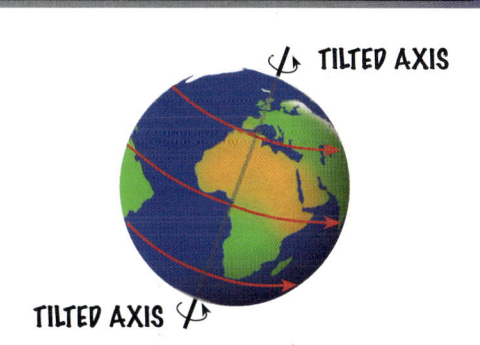

TILTED AXIS

TILTED AXIS

Daytime in Britain occurs when our country faces TOWARDS THE SUN.

Night-time in Britain occurs when our country faces AWAY FROM THE SUN.

APPARENT MOVEMENT OF THE SUN DURING DAYTIME

During daytime the SUN appears to move in a curved path across the sky. This apparent movement occurs because the Earth is rotating around on its axis in one direction creating the impression that the Sun is moving in a curved path in the opposite direction.

At SUNRISE the Sun appears in the sky in an easterly direction.

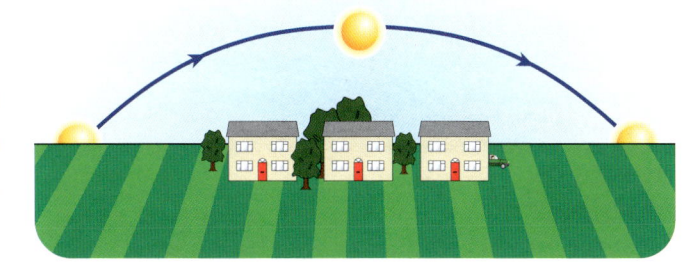

At SUNSET the Sun disappears from the sky in a westerly direction.

THE FOUR SEASONS

The EARTH moves around the SUN in a path called an ORBIT which is a slightly squashed circle. It orbits the Sun once every 365¼ days giving us the four different seasons SPRING, SUMMER, AUTUMN and WINTER. The different seasons occur because the axis of spin of the Earth is at an angle to the Sun.

SPRING

In the SUMMER the Northern Hemisphere is tilted towards the Sun and the weather is usually warm. This is the Northern Hemisphere summer.

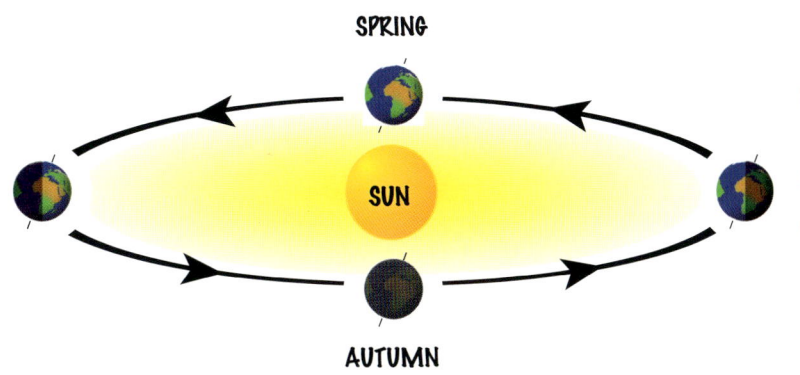

SUN

In the WINTER the Northern Hemisphere is tilted away from the Sun and the weather is usually cold. This is the Northern Hemisphere winter.

AUTUMN

Lonsdale Science Revision Guides

THE EARTH, SUN AND MOON

The Solar System And Beyond — 2

The SUN is a continuous source of light. It is called a LUMINOUS object. The EARTH and MOON do not give out light. They are called NON-LUMINOUS objects. We can see the Moon from the Earth because light from the Sun is reflected from its surface. If we were to stand on the Moon we would see the Earth for the same reason.

PHASES OF THE MOON

At the same time as the Earth is in orbit around the Sun, the Moon is in orbit around the Earth. It takes the Moon 28 days to orbit the Earth once and during this time its appearance changes.

As it orbits the Earth the amount of the Moon's surface which reflects light towards the earth changes. This gives us the different PHASES of the moon.

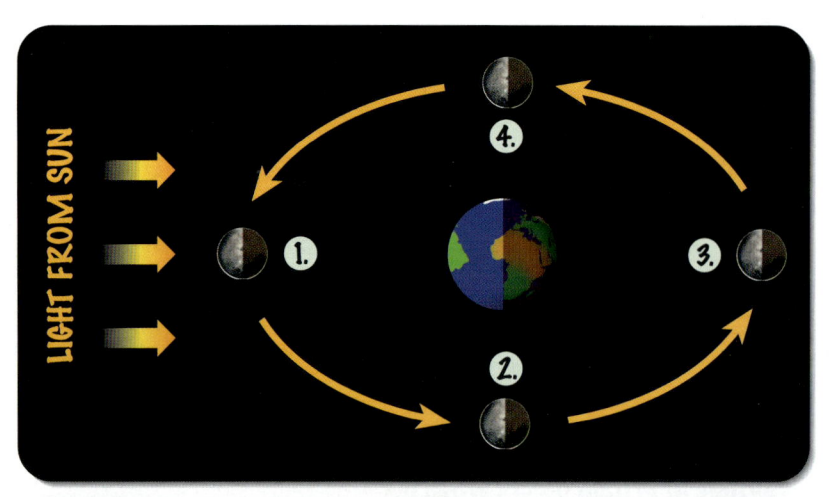

LIGHT FROM SUN

1. NEW MOON
NONE of the Moon's surface which faces the Earth reflects any light towards us.

2. HALF MOON after 7 days
HALF of the Moon's surface which faces the Earth reflects light towards us.

3. FULL MOON after 14 days
ALL of the Moon's surface which faces the Earth reflects light towards us.

4. HALF MOON after 21 days
HALF of the Moon's surface which faces the Earth reflects light towards us.

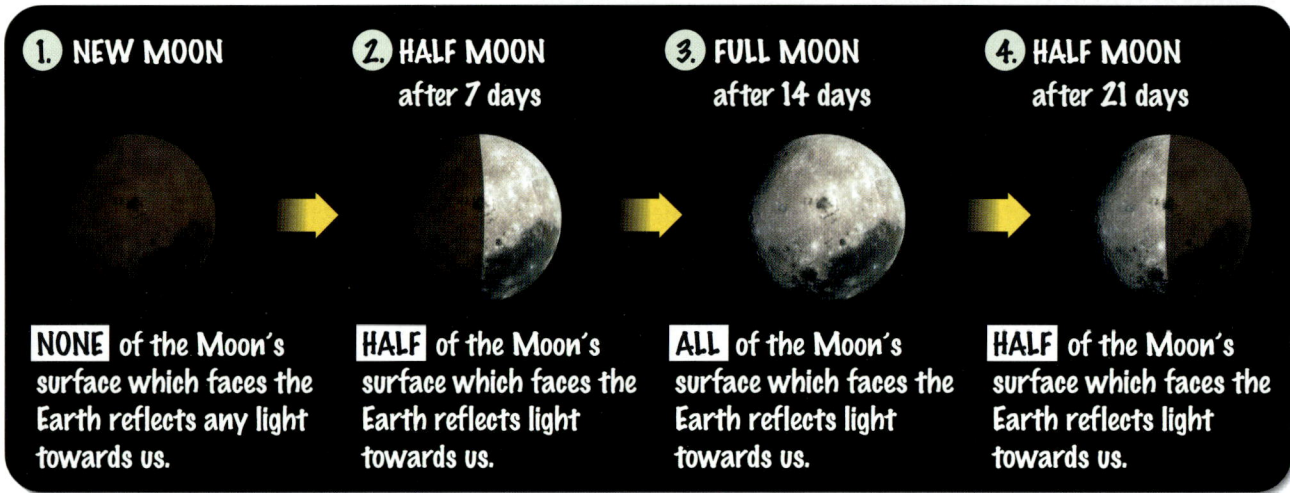

ECLIPSES OF THE SUN AND MOON

An ECLIPSE OF THE SUN occurs when the MOON is in a direct line between the Sun and the Earth. The Moon then BLOCKS LIGHT from the SUN and casts its shadow on the Earth.

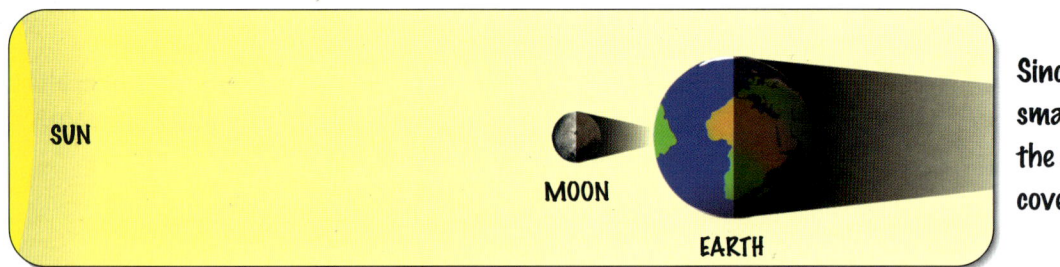

Since the Moon is much smaller than the Earth the shadow it casts only covers part of the Earth.

An ECLIPSE OF THE MOON occurs when the EARTH is in a direct line between the Sun and the Moon. The Earth then BLOCKS LIGHT from the SUN and casts its shadow on the Moon.

Since the Earth is much bigger than the Moon the shadow it casts completely covers all of the Moon.

THE SOLAR SYSTEM

The SOLAR SYSTEM is made up of the SUN in the centre, surrounded by NINE DIFFERENT PLANETS, one of which is the EARTH. All the other planets orbit the Sun in a similar way to the Earth. Like the Earth they do not give out light and we only see them because they reflect light from the Sun.

Between Mars and Jupiter there is a band of rock debris called ASTEROIDS. These asteroids vary in size, with some of them 500km or even more in diameter.

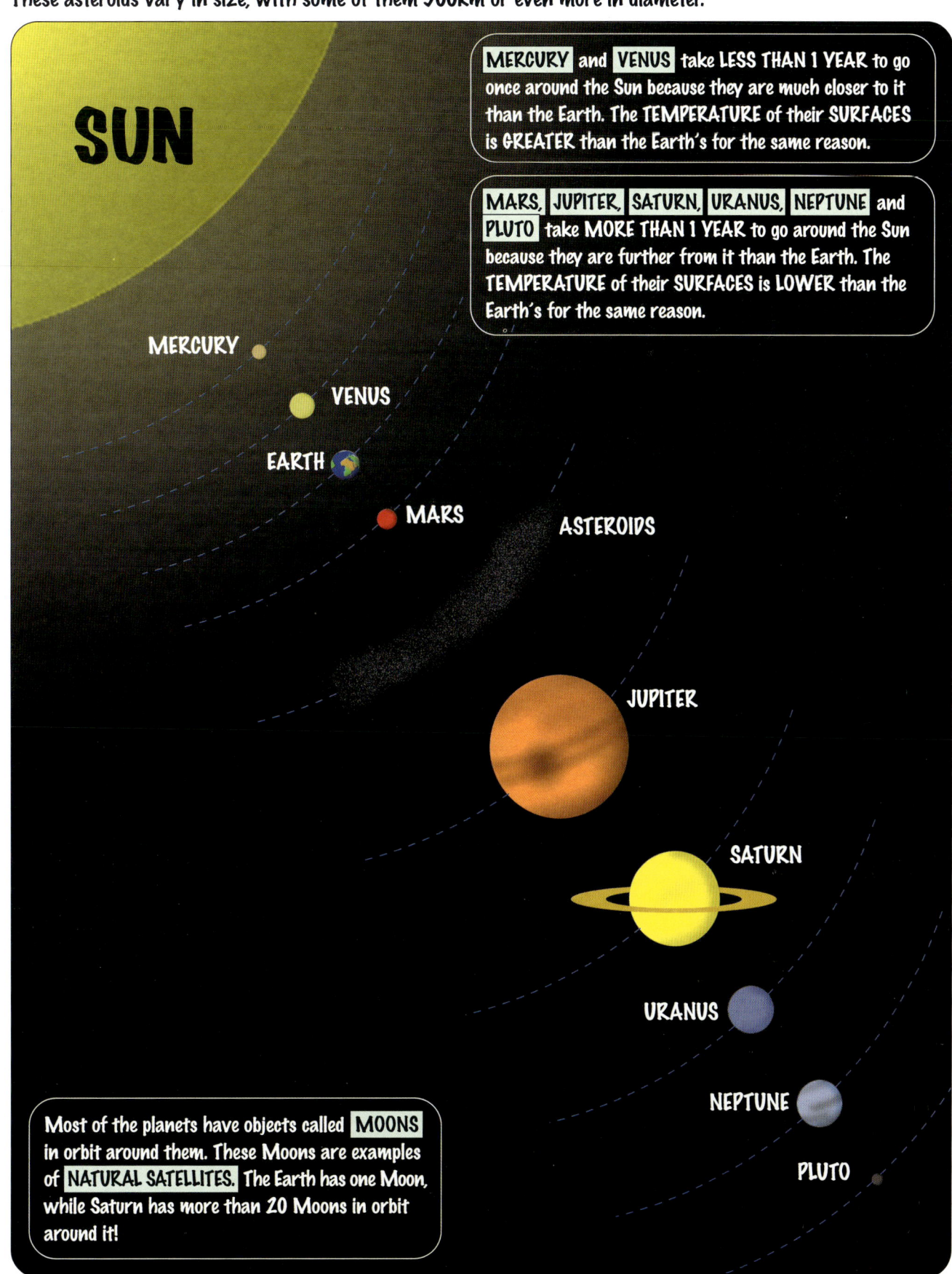

MERCURY and VENUS take LESS THAN 1 YEAR to go once around the Sun because they are much closer to it than the Earth. The TEMPERATURE of their SURFACES is GREATER than the Earth's for the same reason.

MARS, JUPITER, SATURN, URANUS, NEPTUNE and PLUTO take MORE THAN 1 YEAR to go around the Sun because they are further from it than the Earth. The TEMPERATURE of their SURFACES is LOWER than the Earth's for the same reason.

Most of the planets have objects called MOONS in orbit around them. These Moons are examples of NATURAL SATELLITES. The Earth has one Moon, while Saturn has more than 20 Moons in orbit around it!

BEYOND OUR SOLAR SYSTEM

THE SUN AND OTHER STARS

The SUN is ONE STAR out of many millions of stars found in our GALAXY, the MILKY WAY. Like the Sun all stars are sources of light. Beyond our galaxy is the UNIVERSE which is made up of billions of galaxies spread out through space.

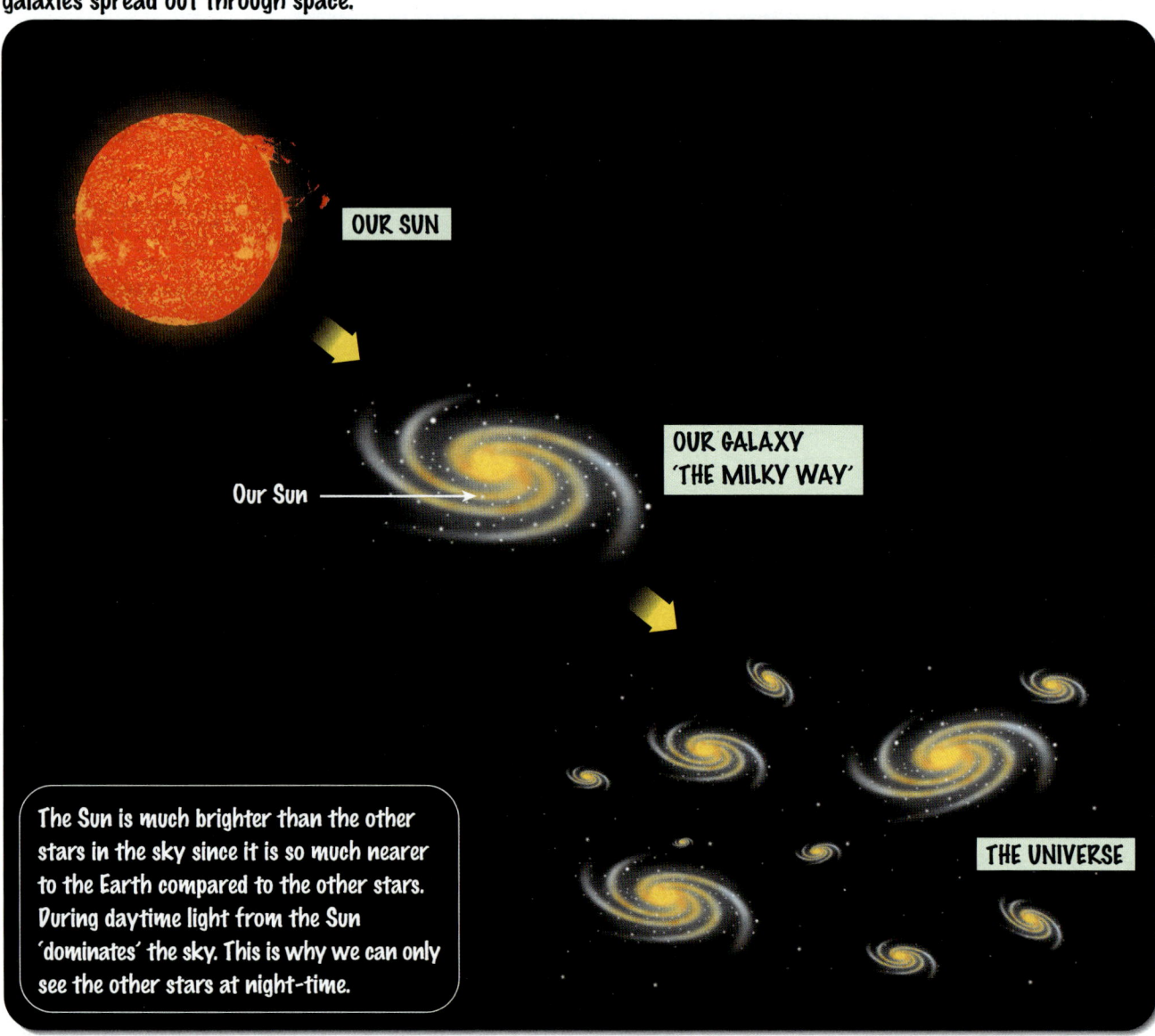

OUR SUN

OUR GALAXY 'THE MILKY WAY'

Our Sun

THE UNIVERSE

The Sun is much brighter than the other stars in the sky since it is so much nearer to the Earth compared to the other stars. During daytime light from the Sun 'dominates' the sky. This is why we can only see the other stars at night-time.

APPARENT MOVEMENT OF THE STARS DURING NIGHT-TIME

During night-time the STARS appear to move across the sky. Just like the movement of the Sun this apparent movement of the stars is also due to the earth rotating around on its axis in one direction. This creates the impression that the stars are moving in the opposite direction.

KEYWORDS AND COMPREHENSION

The Solar System And Beyond — 5

KEYWORDS

Match the keywords from this unit to their definitions ...

EARTH	An object that does not give out light.
ORBIT	Made up of the Sun and the 9 different planets
SEASONS	A planet that completes one rotation every 24 hours
SUN	The path taken by a planet around the sun
NON-LUMINOUS	A luminous object that is a continuous source of light
MOON	This occurs when the Sun, Earth and Moon are all in one direct line
ECLIPSE	These occur because the Earth moves around the Sun
SOLAR SYSTEM	Made up of a billion galaxies
PLANETS	Made up of a million stars
STAR	An object that takes 28 days to orbit the Earth
GALAXY	The Earth is one, Mars is one, Pluto is one and so on
UNIVERSE	Giant luminous object at the centre of the Solar System

ORGANISATION OF OUR SOLAR SYSTEM

Read this passage and then answer the questions below.

For over 2000 years there has been a variety of ideas concerning the organisation of our solar system. It all began in approximately 600 B.C. with Thales who proposed the idea that the Earth was a disc floating on water. Around 500 B.C. Pythagoras then proposed that the Earth was at the centre with all the stars in orbit around it. This model was called the geocentric model and it was accepted by the rulers of Ancient Greece. Some 300 years later Aristarchus proposed that the Sun was at the centre with the Earth in orbit around it. This was called the heliocentric model but it was rejected as he had no experimental support.

In 120 AD Ptolemy proposed an updated geocentric model where the Sun circled the Earth and the other planets circled the Sun. Things then became fairly quiet until the sixteenth century when Copernicus provided experimental support for the heliocentric model. However he did not publish his results until close to his death as they would have challenged the beliefs of the authorities and the church. Galileo then took up on Copernicus' ideas and using a telescope he discovered four moons going around Jupiter which provided evidence for the heliocentric model. Again the church was not impressed and he was jailed for life. Finally Isaac Newton with his theory of gravity and knowledge of the ideas of Galileo proved that Copernicus was correct after all.

1. What is the geocentric model and who was the first to propose it?
2. What is the heliocentric model and who was the first to propose it?
3. Why was the heliocentric model rejected?
4. What did Ptolemy propose in 120 A.D.
5. Copernicus provided experimental support for the heliocentric model. Why did he not publish his results until close to his death?
6. How did Galileo provide evidence for the heliocentric model?
7. Who finally proved that the heliocentric model was correct after all?

Lonsdale Science Revision Guides

TESTING UNDERSTANDING

The Solar System And Beyond — 6

SOLAR SYSTEM

The Earth completes one rotation every .... hours giving us .... and .... Because the Earth is rotating the .... appears to move across the sky during the day. The path of the Earth around the .... is called an .... The Earth takes .... days to complete one of these during which the Earth experiences the four different ....

The Sun is called a .... object since it gives out its own .... The Moon takes 28 days to go around the .... and during this time its appearance changes giving us the different .... occur when the .... , Earth and Moon are all in one direct line and they occur when either the Earth or the Moon casts a .... The nine different .... and the .... is known as the Solar System. Mercury and .... are closer to the Sun than the Earth. This means that they take .... than one year to go around the .... once. All the other planets take .... than one year, except the .... which takes exactly one year.

The .... is made up of billions of galaxies with each one being made up of millions of .... , one of which is the .... The stars appear to move across the .... during the night because the earth is rotating.

ROTATION TIME

The bar chart shows the time taken by five planets A, B, C, D and E in the solar system to complete one rotation.

1. Which planet is Earth? Explain your answer.

2. Neptune takes two-thirds as long as the Earth to complete one rotation. Which planet is Neptune?

3. Uranus takes 1 hour longer than Jupiter to complete one rotation. Which planets are Uranus and Jupiter?

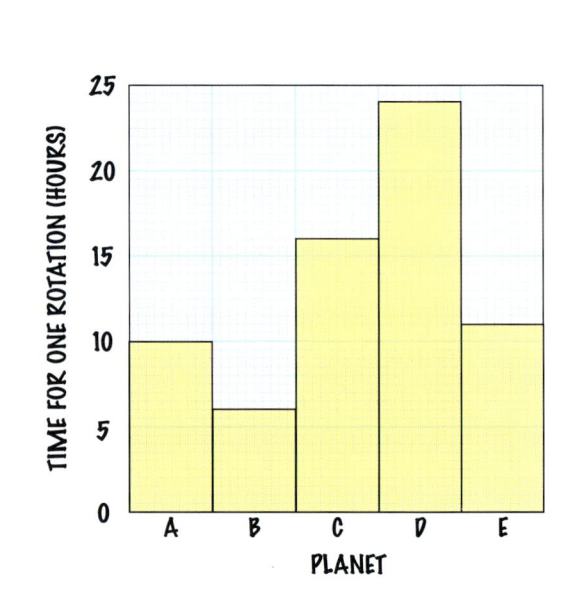

SCIENTIFIC INVESTIGATION

The Solar System And Beyond — 7

A pupil was asked to investigate whether there was a relationship between the time it takes a planet to orbit the Sun and its distance from the Sun. He was given the following data about the innermost planets in the solar system where planet A is the nearest to the Sun and so on.

ORBIT TIME
A = 3 months
B = 7.5 months
C = 12 months
D = 23 months

DISTANCE FROM SUN
(In comparison to the distance of the Earth from the Sun)
A = 0.4
B = 0.7
C = 1.0
D = 1.5

1. Name the planets A, B, C and D.

   A =   B =

   C =   D =

2. On the axes draw a graph of orbit time against distance from Sun.

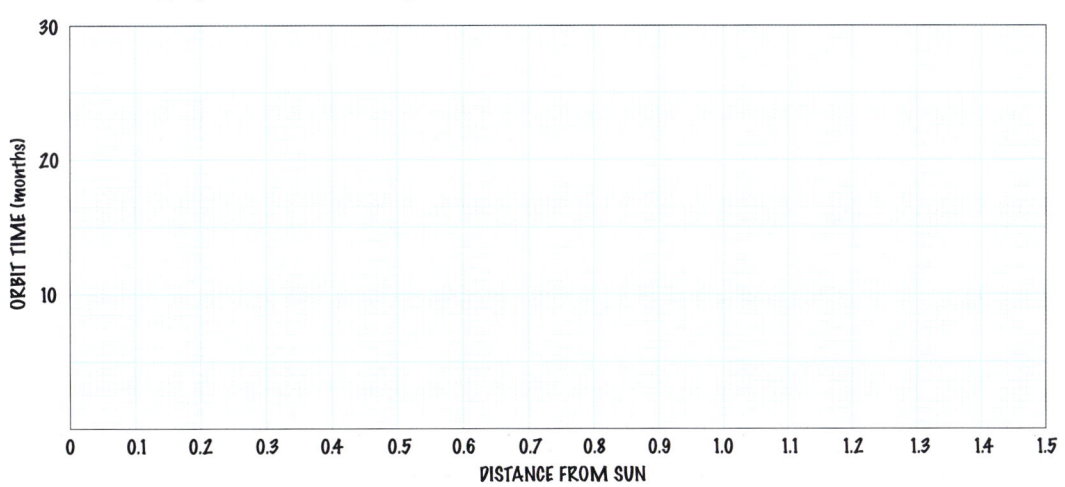

   [Graph: Orbit Time (months) 0–30 on y-axis, Distance from Sun 0–1.5 on x-axis]

3. What relationship is there between orbit time and distance from the Sun?

4. The distance from Jupiter to the Sun is 5.2 times greater than the distance from the Earth to the Sun. Would you expect Jupiter to have an orbit time of above or below 23 months? Explain your answer.

5. A 'tenth' planet has been discovered which has an orbit time of 18 months. Use your graph to calculate its approximate distance from the Sun.

6. Between which two planets does this 'tenth' planet orbit?

Lonsdale Science Revision Guides

INDEX

A
Acceleration 61, 64
Acid 32, 33, 34, 45, 39, 40
Adaptation 18, 19
Adolescence 14
Air resistance 74
Ammeter 68, 69
Amniotic fluid 13, 14
Amphibians 28
Amps 68
Animals 27
Antacid 35
Asteroids 83

B
Balanced forces 74
Battery 67
Biomass 62
Birds 28
Birth 14
Bulb 67, 68
Bunsen burner 60
Burning 41

C
Cable 70
Calories 63
Carbon dioxide, test for 40
Carbon dioxide 40, 41
Carbonates 40
Carnivores 20
Cell division 7, 13
Cell membrane 5, 12
Cell wall 5
Cells 4, 5, 6, 7, 67, 68
Cells, animal 5, 7
Cells, specialist 6
Cells, plant 5, 7
Cervix 12
Chemical reaction 39
Chemicals 61
Chloroplasts 5
Chromatograms 55
Chromatography 55
Classification 26, 27
Coal 42, 60, 61
Combustion 41
Components 67, 68, 69
Condensation 54
Consumers 20
Corrosion 39
Corrosive 33, 34
Cytoplasm 5, 12

D
Daytime 81
Density 75
Diffusion 48
Distance - time graph 77
Distillation 54
Drag 74

E
Earth 81, 82, 83
Eclipse 82
Electric circuits 67
Electric current 67, 68, 69, 70
Embryo 13
Energy 60
Environment 26
Evaporation 54
Expansion 47
Eyepiece lens 4

F
Fertilisation 7, 11, 13
Fertilisation, internal 11
Fertilisation, external 11
Fire safety 41
Fish 28
Foetus 13
Food 63
Food chains 20, 21
Food webs 21
Force 74
Forcemeter 74, 75
Fossil fuels 42, 61
Friction 74, 76, 77
Fuel 41, 42, 62
Fuse 70

G
Galaxy 84
Gas pressure 49
Gases 46, 47, 48
Geothermal 62
Gravity 74

H
Habitats 18
Harmful 33, 34
Hazard symbols 33
Hazcards 33
Heat 41
Herbivores 20
Hibernation 18, 19
Hydrocarbons 42
Hydrogen 39, 40
Hydrogen, test for 39

I
Implantation 13
Indicators 33, 34
Inheritance 26
Insoluble 53
Insulators 18, 19
Invertebrates 27
Irreversible 39
Irritant 33, 34

J
Joules 63

K
Kilocalories 63
Kilograms 74

L
Limewater 40, 42
Liquids 46, 47, 48
Litmus 34
Lubricant 76
Luminous 82

M
Magnification 4
Mains supply 70
Mammals 28
Mass 74, 75
Menstrual cycle 13
Metals 39
Methane 42
Microscope 4
Migration 19
Mineral oil 42, 60, 61
Mixtures 53
Moon 82

N
Natural Gas 42, 60, 61
Nerves 70
Neutral 32
Neutralisation 35
Newtons 74
Night-time 81
Non-luminous 82
Non-renewable 61
Nucleus 5, 12

O
Objective lens 4
Orbit 81
Organs 6
Ovary 12
Oviduct 12
Ovulation 13
Oxides 41
Oxygen 41

P
Parallel Circuit 69
Particle theory 47, 48, 53
Penis 12
pH 32, 34
pH scale 34
Phases 82
Placenta 13, 14
Planets 83
Plants 27
Plastics 61
Plug 70
Pollination 7
Predators 20
Prey 20

R
Producers 20
Products 39

R
Reactants 39
Renewables 62
Reproductive systems 12
Reptiles 26
Resistance 69
Running water 62

S
Saturated solutions 56
Seasons 81
Series circuit 67, 69
Sex cells 12
Solar system 83
Solids 46, 47
Soluble 53, 56
Solute 53
Solutions 53, 56
Solvent 53
Speed 77
Sperm duct 12
Stars 84
Stopping distance 77
Sun 61, 62, 63, 81, 82, 83, 84
Sunlight 62
Switch 67

T
Testes 12
Three states of matter 46
Tissues 6

U
Umbilical cord 14
Universal indicator 34
Universe 84
Upthrust 74, 75
Urethra 12
Uterus 12, 13

V
Vacuole 5
Vagina 12
Variation 25
Vertebrates 27
Volume 75

W
Water 42
Waves 62
Weight 74, 75
Wind 62
Wires 67
Wood 60